Luxembourg

Luxembourg

BY ANN HEINRICHS

*Enchantment of the World
Second Series*

Children's Press®

A Division of Scholastic Inc.

NEW YORK   TORONTO   LONDON   AUCKLAND   SYDNEY
MEXICO CITY   NEW DELHI   HONG KONG
DANBURY, CONNECTICUT

Frontispiece: A castle in Vianden

Consultant: Gerald Newton, PhD, Director, Centre for Luxembourg Studies,
The University of Sheffield, Sheffield, England, UK

Please note: All statistics are as up-to-date as possible at the time of publication.

Book production by Herman Adler Design

Library of Congress Cataloging-in-Publication Data

Heinrichs, Ann.
  Luxembourg / by Ann Heinrichs.
      p. cm. — (Enchantment of the world. Second series)
  Includes bibliographical references and index.
  ISBN 0-516-23681-4
  1. Luxembourg—Juvenile literature. I. Title. II. Series.
  DH905.H45 2005
  949.35—dc22   2004030924

Luxembourg

Contents

CHAPTER

ONE Citizens of the World 8

TWO Mountains, Valleys, and Hills 16

THREE The Green Heart of Europe 28

FOUR The Growth of a Nation 38

FIVE Governing the Grand Duchy 52

SIX The Nation's Wealth 62

SEVEN Staying as We Are 76

EIGHT Spiritual Roots 90

NINE Culture and Traditions 102

TEN Building a Future on the Past 116

Cover photo:
A view of
Clervaux

The Sûre River

Timeline **128**

Fast Facts **130**

To Find Out More **134**

Index **136**

Ice skating is popular with Luxembourgers.

Citizens of the World

8

Emilie strolls into her preschool. Her teacher welcomes her with a cheery *"Gudde Muergen!"*

Max takes a seat in his sixth-grade classroom. His teacher greets him with *"Guten Morgen!"*

Eric is in high school. He and his classmates answer *"Bonjour!"* to their teacher's greetings.

All these children are students in Luxembourg. Their country is trilingual. That is, it carries out its daily business in three languages—Luxembourgish, German, and French. By

Opposite: **Chateau De Beaufort in Luxembourg**

Students in Luxembourg learn about electricity.

the time students finish high school, they have mastered all three languages. Many have developed skills in English, too. They are prepared to work or study almost anywhere in Europe.

Luxembourg is a land of magnificent castles and picturesque villages. For centuries, it has been a crossroads of cultures. Long ago, Celtic and Germanic tribes settled among its river valleys and forested hills. When the Roman emperor Julius Caesar conquered the region in 53 B.C., it became part of the Roman Empire. That ended with an invasion of Frankish tribes. The Franks went on to rule for nearly five

Oude Biezen Castle in Bilzen

LUXEMBOURG

- ● Cities of over 10,000 people
- ○ Other cities
- ✪ National capital

0 ____ 10 miles
0 ____ 10 kilometers

BELGIUM

GERMANY

FRANCE

Troisvierges
Wincrange
Clervaux
Our R.
Wiltz
Our Nature Park
Vianden
Communauté du Lac de la Haute Sûre
Sûre R.
Lake of the Upper Sûre
Heiderscheid
Erpeldange
Bettendorf
Sûre R.
Diekirch
Müllerthal Forest
Haute Sûre Nature Park
Ettelbruck
Echternach
Rambrouch
Bissen
Larochette
Rosport
Redange
Useldange
Mersch
Consdorf
Attert R.
Lintgen
Beckerich
Alzette R.
Junglinster
Mertert
Konstal
Lorentzweiler
Steinfort
Kehlen
Walferdange
Betzdorf
Grevenmacher
Capellen
Strassen
Niederanven
Mamer
Luxembourg City
Wormeldange
Bertrange
Bascharage
Hesperange
Pétange
Sanem
Remich
Differdange
Mondercange
Dalheim
Bettembourg
Bains
Esch-sur-Alzette
Schifflange
Kayl
Dudelange
Moselle Nature Park
Remerschen
Moselle R.

N
W   E
S

hundred years. These many different peoples left their mark on Luxembourg's culture and languages.

Luxembourg is called the Green Heart of Europe. The lush, forested Ardennes Hills cover the northern part of the country. Deep within the shadowy forests are sparkling waterfalls and rushing streams. Luxembourg's Moselle River valley has been a grape-growing region for centuries. Today, it produces some of the finest wines in the world.

Luxembourg has many beautiful castles, such as this one in Clervaux.

As a political unit of its own, Luxembourg is more than one thousand years old. It began as a high, rocky fortress overlooking two river valleys. Counts and dukes of Luxembourg reigned over a territory hundreds of times its present size. Dozens of castles, nestled high on the hillsides, remain from those days.

Over the centuries, Christianity gained a firm foothold in Luxembourg. Roman Catholic churches, festivals, and devotions became a vital force in everyday life. Today, most people in the country remain Catholic, and religious celebrations still energize towns and villages across the countryside.

Notre Dame is one of many Catholic churches in Luxembourg.

Modern Luxembourg is one of the smallest nations in the world. Yet small as it is, it wields great power in the European community and in the world. Luxembourg was a founding member of the European Union (EU), an organization of European nations that cooperate on economic and social policies. Several EU offices now operate out of Luxembourg. Hundreds of international banks are headquartered there, too. Europe's largest steel corporation is based in Luxembourg. So is Europe's largest communications satellite company. In most sectors of the economy, international business is Luxembourg's business.

This international culture is reflected in Luxembourg's people. Today, as in centuries before, Luxembourg is a meeting point for people of many cultures and languages. More than one-third of the people living in Luxembourg were born in other countries.

Luxembourg has an international slant. So it's only natural that Luxembourg's children are well-prepared to live in the world community. They grow up knowing they are citizens of the world.

People enjoy the scenic
Valle de Pretrusse.

Mountains, Valleys, and Hills

L
UXEMBOURG IS A TINY NATION IN NORTHWESTERN EUROPE. It's one of the smallest nations in the world. It covers only about 999 square miles (2,586 square kilometers).

To get an idea of Luxembourg's size, take a look at some comparisons. Luxembourg is smaller than Rhode Island, the smallest U.S. state. It would even fit comfortably inside Montana's Glacier National Park. In fact, *three* Luxembourgs would fit into Yellowstone National Park!

Luxembourg's Neighbors

Luxembourg is shaped a bit like a mitten with a very short thumb. Germany lies to the east of Luxembourg, on the "thumb" side. France is on the south, where the "wrist" would be.

Belgium borders Luxembourg on the north and west. In fact, the part of Belgium that borders Luxembourg is called Belgium's province of Luxembourg. This province is actually bigger than the country of Luxembourg itself! It was once part of the nation of Luxembourg, but it became part of Belgium in 1839.

Opposite: **Alzette Valley**

The River Semois adds beauty to Bouillon.

Luxembourg's Geographical Features

Area: 999 square miles (2,586 square km)

Greatest distance, north–south: 55 miles (89 km)

Greatest distance, east–west: 35 miles (56 km)

Highest elevation: Buurgplaatz, 1,835 feet (559 meters) above sea level

Lowest elevation: 435 feet (133 m) above sea level, along the Moselle River

Major rivers: Moselle, Sûre, Our, and Alzette

Largest lake: Lake of the Upper Sûre

Average January temperature: 33°F (0.8°C) in Luxembourg City

Average July temperature: 63.5°F (17.5°C) in Luxembourg City

Average annual precipitation: 31 inches (79 centimeters)

Luxembourg has also had close ties with The Netherlands, which is north of Belgium. Together, the three are called the Benelux countries. The word *Benelux* was made out of the first few letters of each country's name. In 1960, they banded together to form the Benelux Economic Union. This allowed for the free movement of workers, goods, and money among the three countries. These three nations are also called the Low Countries because their land does not rise very high.

Luxembourg has two main land regions. One is the Oesling Region, which covers the northern portion of the country. It's also called the Ardennes Region because it lies on the slopes of the Ardennes Hills. These hills lie mainly in Belgium and also extend southward into France.

In Luxembourg, the Ardennes Region is a hilly, forested plateau where rivers cut deep valleys into the land. A hill called Buurgplaatz, in the far north, is the country's highest point, at 1,835 feet (559 m). Many old castles are perched among the hills. The castles of Vianden and Clervaux are two of Luxembourg's most visited sites.

Ardennes countryside

Alzette

The Oesling is sparsely populated. It's dotted with villages and small towns that cling to the hillsides or nestle in the valleys. Soil in the Oesling is not naturally rich. But farmers there are able to raise many crops by using fertilizers. They also graze their cattle in the river valleys.

The Bon Pays

The country's other main land region is called the Bon Pays in French and Gutland in German. Both names mean "good land." This is the southern two-thirds of the country, where most of Luxembourg's people and industries are found. The rolling countryside of the Bon Pays is fertile farmland. Luxembourg City, the capital and largest city, is located in the southern part of the Bon Pays.

Southwestern Luxembourg is sometimes called the Land of Red Earth. It's named for the rich, reddish iron-ore deposits once mined there. Esch-sur-Alzette was the region's mining center.

The Moselle Valley runs along Luxembourg's southeastern border. The sunny hillsides of this valley are known for their vineyards, or land where grapevines are grown. In fact, people on both sides of the Moselle have grown grapes since ancient times. Wines made from Moselle Valley grapes are prized around the world.

The Müllerthal, along the east-central border, is known as Luxembourg's Little Switzerland. Like Switzerland, it's a region of rough, craggy mountains. Swift streams rush through the Müllerthal's narrow gorges, making waterfalls as they tumble down the rocks.

The village of Ehnen lies along the Moselle Valley.

Looking at Luxembourg's Towns

Vianden is one of Luxembourg's most visited towns. It rests in the Our River valley among the forested hills of the Ardennes. Vianden's prized site is its huge castle (below). The castle has a maze of rooms that have been restored and decorated in their original style. Museums in town include the Museum of Dolls and Toys, which displays more than five hundred dolls, and the Museum of Rustic Arts. Vianden was also once the home of French author Victor Hugo. His home is now a museum.

Clervaux, in the northern Ardennes Region, is known for its twelfth-century castle. The castle is now a museum that houses several exhibits, including photography by Luxembourg native Edward Steichen. Clervaux's Benedictine abbey sits high in the forested hills above the town. It features an exhibit on life in an abbey, a community where monks or other religious people live.

The small village of Esch-sur-Sûre nestles in a loop of the Sûre River. Steep cliffs rise all around the town. Esch-sur-Sûre is the headquarters for the Natural Park of the Upper Sûre, which surrounds Luxembourg's largest lake. Local attractions include an old candle factory, a cloth-making museum, and the ruins of a castle. Outside of town is the magnificent one thousand-year-old Bourscheid Castle.

Just north of Esch-sur-Sûre is the town of Wiltz, which is known as the capital of the Ardennes. Every summer, the town holds an international music and theater festival on the grounds of its castle.

Echternach (right) is the main town in the Müllerthal Region. It was also the home of Saint Willibrord, one of Luxembourg's most famous religious figures. Willibrord opened Echternach's abbey in the seventh century. The town's attractions include both the abbey and a beautiful basilica, or early Christian church, which contains Saint Willibrord's remains. Echternach's best-known events are its annual dancing procession and its international music festival.

Diekirch is the home of the National Museum of Military History. Its exhibits explore the Battle of the Bulge and other local events during World War II (1939–1945). Diekirch's Museum of Roman Mosaics contains many artifacts from when the Romans controlled Luxembourg, in the first centuries A.D. The fifth-century Church of Saint Laurent was built on the ruins of an ancient Roman villa.

Grevenmacher is the capital of the Moselle Valley wine region. It's the major town along the Route du Vin, or Wine Trail, which winds through the wine-making villages along the Moselle. As in other towns along the route, Grevenmacher's winemakers offer wine tastings and tours of their wine cellars.

Esch-sur-Alzette is Luxembourg's second-largest city. It was once the hub of the nation's mining region, but it declined along with the mining industry. Today, the city has been rebuilt. Many of its buildings are in the art deco style of the 1920s. The city's Museum of the National Resistance highlights Luxembourg's secret opposition to German forces during World War II.

Caves and Caverns

Tucked away in Luxembourg's mountains and valleys are many dark caves and large caverns. They were created over millions of years as water wore away sandstone or limestone rock.

In some caves, scientists have discovered artifacts from ancient human civilizations. Caves in the Black Ernz, White Ernz, and Sûre River valleys reveal the presence of humans tens of thousands of years ago.

Moestroff Cave, near Diekirch, is Luxembourg's largest maze cave. It has nearly 2.5 miles (4 km) of winding tunnels and narrow passageways. Moestroff is an artesian maze cave—one that forms tunnels on many levels.

The Müllerthal Region is famous for its caves. One is Keltenhiel (in Luxembourgish) or Räuberhöhle (in German). To make their way through its entire length, cave explorers must crouch to get through a narrow passageway. Nearby is Nenghis Hiel, which has a narrow opening that leads to a wide chamber. The Grotte Sainte-Barbe cave is strictly for experts. Explorers must climb down ropes to enter it. Their reward is a spectacular view of tall chambers and limestone formations.

Waterways

The Moselle River forms much of Luxembourg's eastern border with Germany. The Moselle continues on to join the Rhine River in Germany. Large ships on the Moselle carry Luxembourg's products to international markets.

The Alzette and Sûre rivers wind through Luxembourg and flow into the Moselle. The Sûre and its tributary the Our form the rest of the eastern border.

The Alzette River has played an important role in Luxembourg's history. A loop in the Alzette surrounds a high, rocky point of land called the Bock. On this natural fortress, Luxembourg had its beginnings as an independent state. The city that grew up around the Bock is today's Luxembourg City.

The Sûre River forms part of Luxembourg's eastern border.

The Lake of the Upper Sûre is Luxembourg's largest lake. It was created when a dam was built on the Sûre River. This lake, high in the Ardennes, provides much of Luxembourg's drinking water. Many other small lakes are scattered throughout the country.

Climate

Luxembourgers enjoy a temperate climate, without sweltering heat or bitter cold. Summers are cool, and winters are mild. Warm weather prevails from May through September. July is the warmest month. Yet even in the summer, nights can be

Durbury

chilly. Northern Luxembourg is generally cooler than the rest of the country. The heaviest winter snows fall high in the Ardennes Hills.

Southwestern Luxembourg gets the most rainfall, while the southeast gets the least. Still, visitors to Luxembourg are advised to bring an umbrella. Most of the country can expect rain on and off throughout the year. The Müllerthal Region is very humid and moist. The skies over the Moselle Valley, on the other hand, are often clear and sunny. This makes the region ideal for both grape farming and recreation.

Harvesting wine grapes is an important job in Luxembourg.

CHAPTER

THREE

The Green Heart of Europe

Luxembourg is called the Green Heart of Europe. The region has been famous for its forests since ancient times. The Roman emperor Julius Caesar wrote about the vast Forest of the Ardennes. This dense woodland stretches through France and Belgium and covers much of Luxembourg. Caesar's enemies sometimes used this forest as a hiding place.

When France took over Luxembourg in 1795, the French named it the Department of Forests. Over the centuries, Luxembourg kept much of its forestland rather than clearing it. Today, forests cover about two-fifths of Luxembourg's land area. Even the capital city is filled with greenery. Towering trees line the streets. In the heart of town, tree-filled parks cover the hillsides of the Pétrusse Valley.

Opposite: **Insenborn on the Sûre River**

Esch-sur-Sûre

Festive Flowers

The Ardennes hillsides around Wiltz are carpeted with broom flowers. On Whit Sunday, seven weeks after Easter, the town celebrates the Broom Flower Festival.

Music and folk dancing fill the streets, and the Broom Flower Queen is crowned. A parade goes through town with floats festooned with the yellow blossoms.

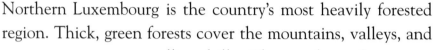

Trees and Flowers

Evergreen trees are common in Luxembourg's northern forests.

Northern Luxembourg is the country's most heavily forested region. Thick, green forests cover the mountains, valleys, and rolling hills. The northern forests are mainly made up of conifers, or cone-bearing trees. They are also known as evergreens because they look green year-round. Norway spruce, Scots pine, and Douglas and silver fir are Luxembourg's most common evergreen trees.

In southern Luxembourg, forests are mainly made up of deciduous, or leaf-shedding, trees. Beeches and oaks are most common there. Other trees native to Luxembourg are ash, willow, and rowan.

Some of Luxembourg's wooded areas are ancient, old-growth forests. Huge trees grow there, many of them more than two hundred years old. One of Europe's oldest forests is in the Ardennes, near Echternach. It has oak, beech, and hornbeam trees.

Another ancient forest lies just outside of Luxembourg City. It's called the Grünwald, or Gréngewald, which means "green forest." This forest is the largest continuous wooded area in Luxembourg. That is, it is the largest area that has not been broken up by roads or human settlement.

Brilliantly colored wildflowers carpet the hillsides in the springtime. Broom flowers grow throughout the Ardennes. These bright yellow flowers are so cheery that the town of Wiltz holds an annual festival in their honor.

People love Luxembourg's broom flowers.

Wild boars are a common sight in the forests of the Ardennes.

Creatures of Forest and Field

The forests of the Ardennes are rich with wildlife. Some of the larger animals are deer, wild boars, and wild sheep. Wild boars roam around in the early morning and at dusk. In the daytime, they sleep in the forest. Wild boars can be pests, as they sometimes eat farmers' crops.

Luxembourg's Natural History

The National Museum of Natural History in Luxembourg City is a fascinating science museum. Each exhibit area fills a massive hall. Visitors first arrive at the exhibit called "Who Am I?" It explores humans in their relation to each other and their surroundings over time. Another exhibit features Luxembourg's various plant and animal habitats. Other halls are devoted to ancient human ancestors, the planet Earth, and the solar system. The museum, located in the city's historic Grund suburb, is a favorite with curious children.

The Butterfly Garden

The Butterfly Garden in Grevenmacher is a huge greenhouse full of beautiful butterflies from around the world. Inside, the climate is kept warm and moist to create an ideal environment for butterflies. The garden's tropical plants were specially chosen to meet the needs of the various butterfly species. In the hatchery, visitors can follow the butterflies' life cycle, from egg to caterpillar to pupa to butterfly.

The forests' smaller animals include squirrels and hedgehogs. Squirrels live both in the forests and in city parks. Rabbits, hares, and red foxes may be seen scurrying across the open fields. Hares are larger than rabbits and have longer ears.

Badgers, polecats, and otters are among Luxembourg's endangered animals. Polecats are declining because they eat

A European brown hare nibbles on a flower.

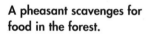
Forest-dwelling badgers

rabbits, which are also becoming more scarce. Badgers have been protected since 1984, so their numbers are increasing. The otter has practically disappeared altogether. Otters can sometimes be seen swimming in the Our River, however.

Birds

Bird-watchers have found almost three hundred bird species in Luxembourg. A few pairs of black storks breed in the northern Ardennes forests. Bird-watchers also search these forests for the rarely seen hazel grouse.

Pheasants, partridges, and woodcocks are more common. They graze for food among the leaves on the forest floor. Shrikes, owls, and wood pigeons are other familiar birds.

A pheasant scavenges for food in the forest.

Lively Gravel Pit

Haff Réimech, in the southern Moselle Valley, is Luxembourg's most important wetland. Gravel used to be dug from this region, and the old gravel pits have become lakes and ponds. Now the site is a protected area and nature reserve.

More than 230 types of birds have been spotted in Haff Réimech. It's the only place in the country where crested grebes (above) and tufted ducks breed. Kingfishers, owls, and woodpeckers breed there, too.

Thousands of graceful, long-legged herons and great white egrets pass through Haff Réimech on their migrations.

Other migrating visitors are raptors, or hunting birds, such as buzzards, kites, and ospreys.

Golden orioles add color to the forest.

Wood pigeons travel in huge flocks of as many as two thousand birds. Many kinds of woodpeckers can be heard hammering on the trees to find insects. Black, green, gray-headed, and spotted woodpeckers all live in the forests.

Wagtails, dippers, and kingfishers are often seen alongside rivers. The southern woodlands and meadows are home to woodlarks, pipits, wheatears, and orioles.

The little stonechat lives in the southwestern forests. It has a reddish orange breast, like a robin. Bird-watchers say its "chat-chat" call sounds like stones crashing together. That's how it got its name.

Luxembourg has set aside several regions as nature parks. The Parc Naturel de la Haute-Sûre (Natural Park of the Upper Sûre) is in northwestern Luxembourg. It surrounds the Lake of the Upper Sûre. Vacationers enjoy boating and swimming in the lake. To ensure that they can enjoy the lake in peace, motorboats are not allowed. The park's headquarters is in the village of Esch-sur-Sûre.

The Natural Park of the Our Valley is in the northeast, and Moselle Nature Park is in Luxembourg's southeast corner. The Germano-Luxembourg Nature Park covers much of northeastern Luxembourg and extends into Germany. It was Europe's first nature park to stretch across national borders.

Amazing views of the Natural Park of the Upper Sûre can be seen from the top of Castle Bourscheid.

The Growth of a Nation

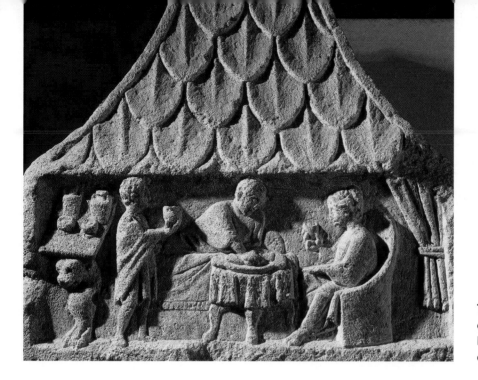

This carving dates back about 1,900 years. It depicts a meal inside a house.

LONG BEFORE RECORDED HISTORY, CELTIC PEOPLE LIVED throughout much of Europe. In Luxembourg, Diekirch was a Celtic stronghold. But Diekirch's story goes back far before the Celts. A huge stone monument called a dolmen still stands in Diekirch. It is called the Deiwelselter, or "Devil's Altar." It looks like a doorway, with tall stacks of stones on the sides and a stone slab across the top. The dolmen dates back to the Middle Stone Age, before the Celts arrived in the region. Ancient people may have used it as a burial site.

A Celtic tribe called the Treveri lived in Luxembourg by the fifth century B.C. Their capital was Trier, just east of the Moselle River. The Roman general Julius Caesar conquered the region in 53 B.C. Then Luxembourg became part of Belgica, a province of the Roman region of Gaul.

Opposite: **Historical attractions such as the Bock casements and bridge date back several centuries.**

Early Luxembourg

■ Roman Empire, A.D. 120
▨ Kingdom of the Franks, A.D. 768
— Holy Roman Empire, A.D. 1250
— Present-day Luxembourg

The Romans built roads, towns, forts, and temples in their new province. They spoke Latin, which became the everyday language of business.

Over the years, invading tribes weakened the Romans' grip. A Germanic tribe called the Franks overtook the region in the A.D. 400s. Then Luxembourg became part of the Frankish kingdom of Austrasia. Under the Frankish kings, the land was divided into counties, each one governed by a count. The count collected taxes, enforced the law, and gathered warriors.

The Franks brought the German language to Luxembourg. They also spread Christianity throughout their kingdom. In 800, Luxembourg became part of the Holy Roman Empire. This vast Christian empire ruled over Europe for more than one thousand years. A great Frankish king named Charlemagne was the first Holy Roman Emperor.

Luxembourg Is Born

The year 963 marks Luxembourg's birth as a state in its own right. That was when Siegfried, the count of Ardennes, acquired an abandoned Roman castle high on a rocky ledge over the Alzette River. From a military standpoint, it was a perfect spot. From here, Siegfried could look out over a broad expanse. He would be protected against surprise attacks, and his soldiers could fire upon enemies from the safety of the high fortifications.

Modern-day Luxembourg City

Siegfried's castle was known as Lucilinburhuc, meaning "little fortress." This is the origin of the name Luxembourg. The settlement that grew up around the castle is now Luxembourg City.

The Bock Casemates

Siegfried's castle stood on a rocky point called the Bock. Not much of the castle remains. One part of the castle that does is the Bock casemates. The casemates are a 14-mile (23-km)-long maze of underground tunnels that served as part of the castle's defenses. The tunnels have openings for firing weapons.

But the casemates don't date all the way back to Siegfried's time. They were built starting in 1713. At one time or another, the casemates housed thousands of soldiers and their horses, as well as workshops, kitchens, bakeries, and slaughterhouses. During World War II, the casemates could shelter up to 35,000 people during bombings or air raids.

Melusina the Mermaid

According to legend, Melusina was the beautiful wife of Count Siegfried, Luxembourg's founder. When Melusina married Siegfried, she had one request. She asked that Siegfried leave her alone in privacy for one day and night a week. Siegfried was only too happy to agree, and thus they lived for many years. Once a week, Melusina withdrew to the tunnels beneath the fortress. She would reappear the next morning.

At last, Siegfried's curiosity got the better of him. One night, he crept down to Melusina's chamber and peeked through the keyhole. To his utter amazement, there lay Melusina in a bathtub with a fish tail draped over the edge. He had married a mermaid!

Melusina could sense that her husband was watching. In one bound, she leapt out the window into the Alzette River below, never to be seen again. In another version of the story, Melusina vanished into the massive rock on which the castle stood. There she knits, making only one stitch a year. When she finishes her knitting, all of Luxembourg will vanish into the rock, too.

The Counts of Luxembourg

Charles IV

Siegfried's descendants, the counts of Luxembourg, extended their realm far beyond the little fortress. Some areas they gained through conquests, while other lands were added by marriages or treaties.

Many great kings and emperors would rise up from Luxembourg. One count became Henry VII, emperor of the Holy Roman Empire. Another count, John the Blind, became king of Bohemia. Bohemia was a kingdom within the Holy Roman Empire. It is now part of the Czech Republic.

When John's son Charles IV was king of Bohemia, he built its city of Prague into a splendid cultural center. Charles became Holy Roman Emperor. It was Charles who made Luxembourg a duchy—a land that is ruled by a duke or duchess. The Luxembourg nobles Wenceslas II and Sigismund also became Holy Roman Emperors.

The European powers all had an eye on Luxembourg. It was attractive because of its great location and the "little fortress" perched on its high lookout point. People compared Luxembourg to the Rock of Gibraltar, a massive rock that overlooks the narrow waterway between the Atlantic Ocean and the Mediterranean Sea. Luxembourg came to be called the Gibraltar of the North.

John the Blind

John the Blind (1296–1346), count of Luxembourg, became Holy Roman Emperor and king of Bohemia. Though he was blind, he was a fearless warrior. He was determined to fight in the Battle of Crécy in 1346 against England's King Edward III. Strapped to his horse, he charged into battle, only to be wounded and die on the battlefield.

John the Blind was popular with his subjects. He started the shepherd's fair that grew into Luxembourg City's Schueberfouer festival. John the Blind's remains are now in Luxembourg City's cathedral (right).

Luxembourg managed to remain independent until 1443. But after that, it was shuffled around from one country to the next for centuries. It belonged to Burgundy, a duchy in present-day France, from 1443 to 1477. Then the Austrian Hapsburg dynasty took Luxembourg over.

Spanish monarchs ruled Luxembourg from 1556 to 1684. It passed to France (1684), Spain (1697), Austria (1714), and then France again (1795). Luxembourgers staged a rebellion against the French in 1798 that was brutally put down.

In 1815, European powers met in the Congress of Vienna. There they decided what to do about Luxembourg. The land of the little fortress would be the independent Grand Duchy of Luxembourg. At the same time, King William I of The Netherlands would be its grand duke.

Life under William was harsh. He charged heavy taxes and treated Luxembourg like his own personal property. In 1830, Luxembourgers helped Belgium revolt against him. After that, both Belgium and William claimed Luxembourg. The conflict was resolved in 1839 by splitting Luxembourg in two.

Divided Luxembourg

United Netherlands, 1815
Land given to Belgium from Luxembourg, 1839
1839 boundaries

Valley of the Seven Castles

The Eisch River valley is called the Valley of the Seven Castles. It covers a small, triangular area northwest of Luxembourg City. These castles were built over a period of several hundred years. Some of the castles are now in ruins.

Septfontaine's castle was built in the 1200s. *Sept fontaines* means "seven springs," and these springs are below the castle. There are two castles of Ansembourg. One was built in the 1100s and the other (above) in the 1600s. The castle of Hollenfels, built in the 1700s, perches high on a cliff top. It's now a youth hostel. The castle of Mersch, first built in the 1100s, stands near the remains of a Roman villa. Other castles in the valley are Koerich and Schoenfels.

Western Luxembourg was largely French-speaking, while people in the east spoke Luxembourgish. This made for a convenient dividing line. As part of Belgium's independence agreement, western Luxembourg went to Belgium. This region is now Belgium's province of Luxembourg. The remaining part of Luxembourg was given a certain amount of independence.

The Place d'Armes is in Luxembourg City.

An Independent Nation

Technically, Luxembourg still belonged to The Netherlands. For the most part, however, the little duchy was left alone to rule its own affairs. But several nations still had their eye on Luxembourg. France was interested in it. So was Prussia, a state that would soon become part of the new country of Germany. The European powers met again in 1867 to decide Luxembourg's fate. This time, the duchy was declared to be absolutely independent and forever neutral—that is, it would take no sides in international wars.

By this time, Luxembourg was enjoying an economic boom. Iron mining in the southwest led to a thriving steel industry. The belching smokestacks of steel plants loomed over Esch-sur-Alzette, Differdange, Dudelange, Pétange, and other southwestern cities.

Luxembourg got a new grand duke in 1890. He was Adolf of the House of Nassau, a region of Germany. Descendants of the House of Nassau have been Luxembourg's monarchs ever since.

After many centuries of being ruled by one power or another, Luxembourgers were gaining a strong sense of national identity. They began to see themselves as a nation of proud, independent people, united in common goals.

World Wars and Occupations

Luxembourg's national spirit faced a serious threat during World War I (1914–1918). German troops marched into Luxembourg in August 1914 and occupied the country until the end of the war. Grand Duchess Charlotte took the throne in 1919. She proved to be a strong, well-loved leader. She helped her nation heal and guided it through the next forty-five years.

The Nazis once controlled Luxembourg.

Things went badly for Luxembourg again during World War II (1939–1945). German troops swept across Europe, swallowing up one nation after another. In one day—May 10, 1940—the Germans marched across Luxembourg and into Belgium, taking control of both countries. By June, they

The Battle of the Bulge was fought in the forests of the Ardennes.

had France in their grip. The grand duchess and her family fled the country for safety.

Under German occupation, Luxembourg became a supply post and command center under a German commander. All French words in the Luxembourgish language were banned. It also became illegal to speak French outside of school. People's names were changed to German names, and Luxembourgers were hounded to embrace their "German motherland." Luxembourgers bitterly resented this.

Meanwhile, the Allied forces opposing Germany were secretly planning to take Europe back. The Allies included Great Britain, France, the United States, and many other countries. In June 1944, Allied troops landed at Normandy, on the French coast. They liberated France and pushed on into Belgium. Luxembourg was freed from German control in September 1944.

The Battle of the Bulge

Liberation did not end Luxembourg's troubles, for the Germans were planning a counterattack.

German troops crossed Luxembourg once again. They made their way through the dense forest of the Ardennes, knowing the Allies would never expect an attack from there.

The Germans were right. Their attack on December 16, 1944, took the Allies completely by surprise. This began the monthlong Battle of the Bulge. This fierce, bloody battle raged across the forests and hills of the Ardennes in Belgium and northern Luxembourg.

The tide began to turn when U.S. general George Patton swung through Luxembourg to attack the Germans from the south. Patton's troops weakened them with one strike after another. By mid-January, the Germans were in retreat. Four months later, they surrendered to the Allies, and the war in Europe was over.

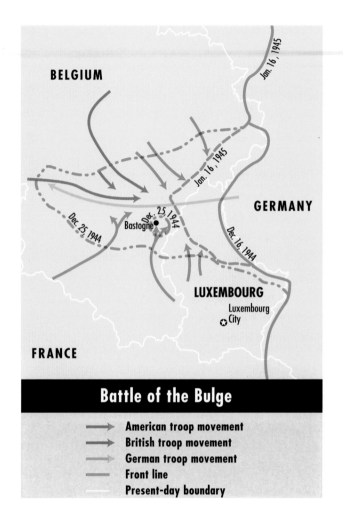

Battle of the Bulge

→ American troop movement
→ British troop movement
→ German troop movement
— Front line
— Present-day boundary

Honoring the Fallen

Just outside of Luxembourg City, near the village of Hamm, is the American Military Cemetery. It's the burial place for thousands of U.S. soldiers killed in the Battle of the Bulge. Among the dead are 101 unknown soldiers and 22 pairs of brothers. One of the cemetery's simple, white crosses marks the grave of General George S. Patton. He survived the war, only to be killed in a car accident in Germany.

The Founding Father

Robert Schuman (1886–1963) is considered the founding father of the European Union. He was born in Luxembourg City's Clausen neighborhood, and he eventually moved to France. There he would hold many high offices, including foreign minister.

In 1950, Schuman proposed the Schuman Plan for economic and military cooperation among European nations. This plan became the basis for the European Coal and Steel Community. It was the first of many alliances that led to the formation of the European Union.

The house where Schuman was born now houses the Robert Schuman Center for European Studies and Research.

Forming a United Europe

Luxembourgers emerged from the long war years with an even greater sense of solidarity. Right away, Luxembourg began taking an active role in international affairs. In 1945, it became a founding member of the United Nations (UN). This is an organization of countries around the world committed to solving conflicts peacefully. Luxembourg also helped form the North Atlantic Treaty Organization (NATO) in 1949. NATO is a military alliance made up of the United States, Canada, and many European nations.

Luxembourgers believed that national borders should not be like solid walls. Instead, European countries could benefit

The Maastricht Treaty

The Maastricht Treaty, or Treaty on European Union, went into effect in 1993. It established the European Union (EU) among its member states. Before that, they had been bound together as the European Economic Community (EEC). Members of the EU agreed to cooperate on economic, environmental, and social policies. They also agreed to introduce the euro as a common currency.

by cooperating among themselves. With Belgium and The Netherlands, Luxembourg formed an economic agreement to trade freely with one another. This alliance became the Benelux Economic Union.

Luxembourg was a driving force in establishing the European Coal and Steel Community (ECSC) in 1952. The country was also a founding member of the European Economic Community (EEC) in 1957. These alliances would pave the way for today's European Union (EU). The EU's European Court of Justice and Council of Ministers are now headquartered in Luxembourg City. The European Parliament's secretariat, or staff, has its offices there, too.

Throughout the centuries, Luxembourg has endured many changes. It has seen its power rise and fall, its lands occupied, and its borders shrink. Yet today it stands proudly as one of Europe's strongest, most influential forces.

The European Union

In 2003, the fifteen members of the EU were Austria, Belgium, Denmark, Finland, France, Germany, Greece, Ireland, Italy, Luxembourg, The Netherlands, Portugal, Spain, Sweden, and the United Kingdom. Ten more nations joined in 2004, raising the total to twenty-five. The new members are Cyprus, the Czech Republic, Estonia, Hungary, Latvia, Lithuania, Malta, Poland, Slovakia, and Slovenia.

Governing the Grand Duchy

L uxembourg's official name is the Grand Duchy of Luxembourg. Its form of government is a constitutional monarchy. That means it has a constitution, or basic set of ruling principles. It also has a monarch—a supreme ruler who reigns over the land.

Opposite: **The Grand Ducal Palace**

The Grand Duchy

Luxembourg's monarch is a grand duke or grand duchess. This is why the country is called a grand duchy. In fact, Luxembourg is the only grand duchy in the world!

Duchess Charlotte attends a session of Luxembourg's parliament.

Luxembourg's rulers belong to a very old family called the House of Nassau. The monarchy stays within that family. Traditionally, when a grand duke or duchess dies or steps down, the throne passes to the oldest son. If there is no son, the oldest daughter ascends to the throne.

Grand Duchess Charlotte abdicated, or stepped down from the throne, in 1964. She had reigned for forty-five years. Her son became Grand Duke Jean. He, in turn, abdicated in 2000 at the age of seventy-nine. Then his oldest son became Grand Duke Henri.

Grand Duke Henri

His Royal Highness Grand Duke Henri (1955–) is the youngest monarch in Europe. After attending secondary schools in Luxembourg and France, he obtained a degree in political science at the University of Geneva, Switzerland. There he met Maria Térèsa Mestre, whom he married in 1981. She is now Grand Duchess Maria Térèsa and the mother of their five children.

The grand duke served on Luxembourg's Council of State from 1980 to 1998. There he became familiar with the national parliament and other government functions. His father, Grand Duke Jean, gave him broad powers in 1998 before stepping down and giving Henri the throne in 2000. Today, Grand Duke Henri is actively involved in environmental issues and drug-abuse prevention among young people.

National Day

Luxembourg's National Day, June 23, celebrates the monarch's birthday. This festival has a long history. The ruling monarch's birthday has been a holiday since the 1700s. Grand Duchess Charlotte's birthday fell on December 23. Usually the holiday was celebrated on the monarch's actual birthday. But because 1961 had an especially harsh winter, the celebration was moved to June 23. Even after Charlotte's reign, that date has remained the official celebration of the royal birthday.

Members of Luxembourg's parliament meet in the Kadenauer Building.

The Parliament

Luxembourg's lawmaking body, or parliament, has only one chamber. It is called the Chambre de Députés, or Chamber of Deputies. Its sixty members are elected for a five-year term. They are elected by voters from each of three districts. All citizens are required to vote, beginning at age eighteen.

In addition, there is a twenty-one-member Conseil d'État (Council of State). The monarch appoints its members for life. They are mainly advisers, but they are sometimes called upon to take part in lawmaking.

Executive Powers

The grand duke or duchess is Luxembourg's head of state. He or she

NATIONAL GOVERNMENT OF LUXEMBOURG

Executive Branch

GRAND DUKE OR GRAND DUCHESS

PRIME MINISTER

COUNCIL OF MINISTERS

Legislative Branch

CHAMBER OF DEPUTIES
(SIXTY MEMBERS)

Judicial

SUPERIOR COURT OF JUSTICE

ADMINISTRATIVE COURT

CONSTITUTIONAL COURT

DISTRICT COURTS

JUSTICES OF THE PEACE

The National Flag

Luxembourg officially adopted its national flag in 1972, but it has been used since the 1800s. The flag consists of three horizontal stripes—red, white, and light blue. It is similar to the flag of The Netherlands, Luxembourg's former ruler, except that Luxembourg's blue stripe is lighter. This set of colors dates from the 1200s. They match the colors on Count Henry V's coat of arms.

National Anthem of Luxembourg

Ons Héemécht ("Our Homeland")
Words by Michel Lentz, music by Jean-Antoine Zinnen; adopted in 1895

> Where the Alzette slowly flows,
> The Sura plays wild pranks,
> Where fragrant vineyards amply grow
> On the Moselle's banks;
> There lies the land for which we would
> Dare everything down here,
> Our own, our native land which ranks
> Deeply in our hearts.
>
> O Thou above, Whose powerful hand
> Makes states or lays them low,
> Protect this Luxembourger land
> From foreign yoke and woe.
> Your spirit of liberty bestow
> On us now as of yore.
> Let freedom's sun in glory glow
> For now and evermore.

represents Luxembourg in formal relations with other countries. In theory, the monarch has the right to organize the government and appoint all its ministers. In practice, however, the monarch does not have wide-ranging executive powers. These powers rest with the Council of Ministers, or cabinet.

The cabinet is made up of the prime minister and several other ministers. They oversee various government concerns, such as health, education, and the environment. All ministers report to the parliament.

The prime minister is the head of government and oversees the day-to-day workings of the country. The monarch appoints the prime minister and the other ministers. But these appointments are usually a ceremonial stamp of approval. The ministers are representatives of the leading political parties in the parliament.

The Courts

Judges on all levels are appointed for life by the monarch. Luxembourg does not have a system of trial by jury. Instead, guilt or innocence is decided by a majority vote of the judges in a court.

Jean-Claude Juncker

Jean-Claude Juncker (1954–) grew up in Luxembourg's southern mining region, where his father worked in a steel plant. He was active in the Christian Social Party and became its president in 1990. Juncker has been deeply involved in promoting unity among European nations. He was governor of the World Bank from 1989 to 1994 and served as chairman of the European Community's council of ministers in 1991.

Juncker assumed many important positions in 1995. He became Luxembourg's prime minister, as well as minister of state and minister of finance. On the European scene, he became governor of the International Monetary Fund (IMF) and governor of the European Investment Bank. He was reaffirmed prime minister in 1999 and 2004.

There are three high courts. The Superior Court of Justice hears appeals from lower courts. The Administrative Court rules on matters relating to civil and social policies. The Constitutional Court decides whether a law is in line with the constitution.

On the next level are two district courts. They handle serious civil, criminal, and business-related cases. The lowest courts are the three justices of the peace. They deal with less important cases.

Regional and Local Government

For regional government, Luxembourg is divided into three districts—Luxembourg, Diekirch, and Grevenmacher. Each is headed by a commissioner.

The districts are divided into twelve cantons, which are further divided into 118 communes or municipalities. Voters in each commune elect a mayor and council. They are responsible for local activities such as health and education.

Foot traffic abounds outside the municipal building in Luxembourg City.

Walking Through Luxembourg City

Luxembourg's capital city grew up around the fortress built by Siegfried, count of Ardennes, in 963. The fortress sat on a high, rocky cliff overlooking the Pétrusse and Alzette rivers. Today that cliff, the Bock, is part of the capital's old town. A pedestrian walkway, the Chemin de la Corniche, winds along the edge of the cliff.

People get around the old town mainly on foot. Much activity revolves around the Old Fish Market and two town squares—Place d'Armes and Place Guillaume II. Highlights of the old town include Notre Dame Cathedral, the Luxembourg City Historical Museum, and the Grand Ducal Palace, home to the royal family.

South of the old town, bridges span the Pétrusse River. The steep hillsides of the Pétrusse Valley are now parklands full of trees and flowers. To the east, the old town's high cliff drops sharply down to the Grund district. Once a working-class neighborhood, it's now an area of fashionable townhouses and shops. Adjoining suburbs are Clausen and Pfaffenthal.

To the northeast, the red Pont (Bridge) Grand-Duchesse Charlotte leads to the European Center on the Kirchberg Plateau. Among its modern, high-rise buildings are many banks, as well as the EU's European Center and European Court of Justice. This district is also home to the National Sports and Cultural Center. Next to it is the Central Park, with a beautifully landscaped lake.

Quick Facts about Luxembourg City

Population: 77,325 (2004)
Year founded: A.D. 963
Founder: Siegfried, count of Ardennes
Average January temperature: 31.1°F (–0.5°C)
Average July temperature: 62.6°F (17°C)
Average annual rainfall: 30.8 in. (78.2 cm)
Annual city festival: Schueberfouer, late August/early September

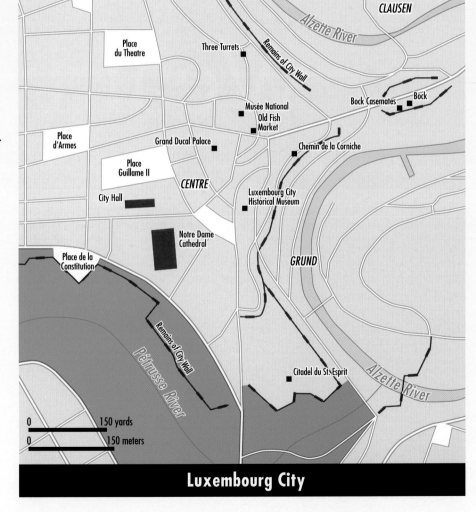

Luxembourg City

The Nation's Wealth

BANQUE
DE LUXEMBOU

LUXEMBOURGERS ENJOY A HIGH STANDARD OF LIVING. THE national income, when averaged per person, was $39,171 a year in 2002. That was the highest average income in the world!

Another stunning figure is Luxembourg's gross domestic product (GDP). That's the value of all goods and services a country produces in a year. Again, per person, Luxembourg held the 2002 world record. It came to $44,588 per person.

A Banking Haven

More than three out of four workers in Luxembourg hold service jobs. This is a much higher share of service workers than other countries have. The reason is banking. Luxembourg is

Opposite: **Luxembourg is a tiny but wealthy country that is home to many banks.**

Policemen on motorcycles

Pictures on the Euro

All euro banknotes, or paper money, have pictures of windows or gateways on the front. This symbolizes the European spirit of openness and cooperation. On the back of each note is a picture of a bridge. This symbolizes the cooperation between Europe and the rest of the world.

Money Facts

The Luxembourg franc used to be the national currency. Like other countries in the European Union, however, Luxembourg switched to the euro on January 1, 2002. The euro is divided into 100 cents. In April 2005, 1 euro was equal to US$1.30, and US$1.00 was equal to 0.769 euros.

one of the largest financial centers in the world. Banking and financial services are Luxembourg's biggest industry. This tiny country has more than 180 banks.

Luxembourg, like Switzerland, is an appealing place to put one's money. Its banks offer two irresistible benefits. One is tax-free returns. No taxes are charged on earnings such as interest and dividends. The other benefit is banking secrecy. Luxembourg's banks refuse to reveal the identity of their customers or the amount of money they hold. By placing money in a Luxembourg bank, a wealthy person or company can avoid paying thousands—or even millions—of dollars in taxes every year!

This may seem too good to be true. Actually, some changes are taking place in Luxembourg's banking laws. For example, Luxembourg has agreed to cooperate with U.S. tax officials in identifying investors guilty of tax fraud.

Also, the EU is considering passing banking laws that would apply to all member nations. One law would place a tax on savings. Most of that tax would go to the saver's home country. Other laws could put an end to banking secrecy.

Of course, many Luxembourgers oppose these measures. They feel that the new laws would hurt the country's economy because so many investors would take their money elsewhere. Others believe that banking reform would have little effect in the long run. They point out that Luxembourg's banks are still appealing because their services are so quick, efficient, and free of red tape.

Beyond Iron and Steel

Mining used to be a big industry in Luxembourg. Iron ore was mined from rich deposits in the southwestern corner of the country. In 1879, Luxembourg began using the Bessemer process to make iron into steel. Then the steel industry grew to become a leading part of the economy.

The Bessemer steel process made steel production a leading industry in Luxembourg.

This was true for a century. Then the worldwide steel industry declined in the 1970s, and Luxembourg's steel production slumped as well. Also, the country's once-rich iron deposits were mined out by the 1980s. Since then, Luxembourg has varied its manufacturing to include foods, chemicals, and glass. Many factories make metal goods such as machines and rubber items such as tires. The country also expanded its banking industry.

The steel industry is still a vital force in the economy, though. In fact, Luxembourg's Arcelor company is the world's largest steelmaking group. It was formed in 2001 through the merger of steel companies in Luxembourg, France, and Spain.

Guy Dolle, CEO of Arcelor, the world's largest steel maker

Inventors

Henri Tudor (1859–1928) was an engineer born in Luxembourg. He developed a lead storage battery called the Tudor accumulator. It was a forerunner of the lead-acid batteries used in cars today.

William J. Kroll (1889–1973) was another Luxembourg native. He was the first to develop a process for taking the metal titanium from its natural state and making it into useful products. Thanks to his Kroll Process, it became possible to make jet engines, artificial hips and knees, and much more. Kroll (second from left) moved to the United States in 1940. He was inducted into the U.S. Inventors Hall of Fame in 2000.

What Luxembourg Grows, Makes, and Mines

Agriculture

Beef and pork (2001)	27,200 metric tons
Barley (1998)	63,200 metric tons
Wheat (1998)	60,100 metric tons

Manufacturing (2001)

Crude steel	2,725,000 metric tons
Rolled steel products	3,990,000 metric tons
Wine	13,480,000 liters

Mining

Luxembourg has no significant commercial mining activity.

Cattle grazing in a pasture

Farming: A Family Affair

Most farming in Luxembourg takes place on small, family-owned farms in the Bon Pays region. Less than 2 percent of the labor force works in agriculture. Beef and dairy cattle account for the most farm income. They provide meat, as well as milk, which is made into butter and cheese. Some farms also keep pigs, chickens, sheep, and horses. Most farmers raise both livestock and crops. The major field crops are barley, wheat, oats, and potatoes.

Grapes are the country's most important fruit. Luxembourg's Moselle wine is made from grapes grown in the Moselle River valley. The vineyards are planted on hillsides along the river.

Cross-Border Workers

Every day, tens of thousands of workers travel from other countries to work in Luxembourg. They're called cross-border workers. In 2002, cross-border workers held more than 37 percent of the jobs in Luxembourg. Most come from France, Belgium, or Germany. This commuting labor force is both an advantage and a disadvantage for Luxembourg.

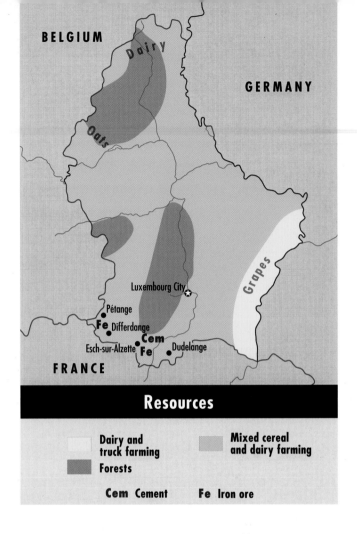

Resources

Dairy and truck farming	Mixed cereal and dairy farming
Forests	

Cem Cement   **Fe** Iron ore

BELGIUM

GERMANY

FRANCE

Dairy

Oats

Grapes

Luxembourg City

Pétange

Fe Differdange

Cem

Esch-sur-Alzette Fe

Dudelange

Grapes are an imporant part of Luxembourg's economy.

On the positive side, cross-border workers help the country thrive economically. They also provide a cushion against shifts in the economy. If people have to be laid off, Luxembourg's residents can be spared. That keeps the unemployment rate low. If more jobs suddenly open up, cross-border workers can fill them.

On the other hand, when these workers retire, they receive pensions, or retirement income, from Luxembourg. But since they live in other countries, they spend that money outside of Luxembourg. Pensions in Luxembourg are very high. For many workers, pensions are equal to about seven-eighths of the salary they had when they retired. That's a lot of money leaving the country.

Luxembourg is trying to combat this money drain. One tactic is to develop the country's high-tech industries. Compared to other types of manufacturing, these industries produce a higher income with a smaller labor force. The idea is that Luxembourgers can fill those jobs without the need to bring in cross-border workers. A growing high-tech industry would also make Luxembourg less dependent on banking.

What Luxembourgers Buy

Luxembourgers' spending habits have changed over the years. The following figures illustrate those changes. They show how much of a household's total spending has gone to various areas.

	1965	1984	2002
Food and drink	47.5%	36.3%	19.7%
Transportation and communication	6.7%	13.1%	18.8%
Leisure, entertainment, education, and culture	6.0%	6.0%	10.8%

Several companies in Luxembourg are now making computers and other electronics.

Air travel is popular in Luxembourg.

Travel and Shipping

People can easily get to Luxembourg from other countries, no matter how they like to travel. Findel Airport, just outside the capital, is Luxembourg's international airport. Luxair is the national airline, and many other nations' airlines fly into Findel. Luxembourg's Cargolux airline transports freight to countries around the world.

Luxembourg keeps its roadways in good repair. Roads range from expressways and national highways to out-of-the-way country roads. Within Luxembourg City, it's often easiest to get around by walking or taking a bus.

Luxembourg has its share of busy roads and expressways.

Taking the bus saves time and money in Luxembourg.

Luxembourg has an extensive bus system. The capital has its own city buses, and bus lines run to many towns throughout the country. Buses also shuttle between the airport and Luxembourg City's train station.

A north–south passenger train runs from Luxembourg City to Clervaux in the far north and Bettembourg in the south.

Another train runs between the capital and towns in the Moselle Valley. Other rail lines continue on to France, Belgium, and Germany.

Goods are shipped in and out of the port of Mertert, on the Moselle River. The Moselle joins the Rhine River in Germany. From the Rhine, Luxembourg's goods can reach many points in western Europe, as well as ports on the North Sea.

Train travel is popular in Luxembourg and throughout the rest of Europe.

The Great 208

Back before there was television, people huddled around their radios to hear music and news. For millions of Europeans, Radio Luxembourg was their link to the outside world. It offered radio shows in English, French, German, Belgian, Dutch, Italian, and many other languages. People tuned in for the latest pop music, as well as talk shows, quiz shows, and news. In Great Britain, Luxembourg's station was "The Great 208." Kids who grew up with 208 still remember hearing their first Elvis Presley and Beatles tunes there.

When TV came along in the 1950s, the station was quick to expand into the new medium. Now called the Radio Télévision Luxembourg (RTL) Group, it operates dozens of

These Luxembourg offices house the RTL Group.

stations in eight countries. Another Luxembourg-based media giant is Société Européenne des Satellites (SES) Global. It's Europe's biggest satellite TV broad-caster, with thirteen powerful ASTRA satellites in orbit. Several other stations are aimed at local Luxembourg audiences.

It's no surprise that Luxembourg welcomed electronic communication. There are almost as many cell phone subscribers in the country as there are people. More than half the population are Internet users, too.

Most daily newspapers in Luxembourg are in German or French or both. *d'Wort/La Voix du Luxembourg* has the most readers. Other important dailies are the *Lëtzebuerger Journal* and *Tageblatt/Zeitung fir Lëtzebuerg*. *The Luxembourg News* and *352* are weekly English-language newspapers. (The name *352* comes from the country code for making interna-tional phone calls to Luxembourg.)

An Astra satellite of the Luxembourg-based SES Global

Staying as We Are

LUXEMBOURG'S NATIONAL MOTTO IS, "WE WANT TO STAY as we are." This is a bold and proud declaration of national identity. But there are many sensitive issues involved in "staying as we are." Ethnic Luxembourgers form the core of the country's population. They originated from a mixture of the many peoples who lived in the region centuries ago. Yet Luxembourg is a multicultural nation, with a diversity of nationalities and languages.

Opposite: **Young Luxembourgers have a strong sense of identity and patriotic pride.**

Luxembourgers come from many different cultural and ethnic backgrounds.

People flock to the Place d'Armes in Luxembourg City.

About 462,690 people live in Luxembourg, according to 2004 estimates. That's a smaller population than the city of Cleveland, Ohio. In the year 2000, thirty-four cities in the United States had a population larger than the entire country of Luxembourg!

Luxembourg's population may be small, but remember—its land area is tiny. An average of 454 people live on every square mile (175 per sq km). In contrast, the United States averages about 80 people per square mile (31 per sq km).

A Nation of City Dwellers

Luxembourgers are spread out very unevenly in their country. Northern Luxembourg is lightly populated. Most people live in the south. That's where the largest cities and busiest industries are. In 2000, 92 percent of Luxembourgers lived in urban areas. As in other countries, more and more people are leaving rural areas and moving to the cities.

Population of Major Cities (2004 est.)

City	Population
Luxembourg City	77,325
Esch-sur-Alzette	27,891
Differdange	18,891
Dudelange	17,514
Pétange	14,382

Luxembourg City is the capital and largest city. Second in size is Esch-sur-Alzette, in the far southwest. It once flourished as an iron and steel center. So did the next-largest cities, which are all in the southwest—Differdange, Dudelange, and Pétange.

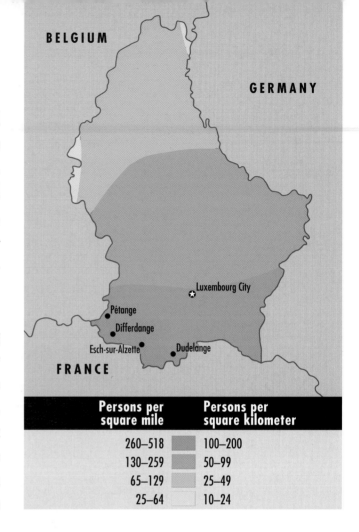

Persons per square mile		Persons per square kilometer
260–518		100–200
130–259		50–99
65–129		25–49
25–64		10–24

Immigrants

Luxembourg's population is growing very slowly. The country has a low birth rate. Every year, about twelve babies are born per thousand people. The worldwide growth rate is about twenty-one per thousand. Yet the economy is growing, which creates a growing need for workers. Immigrants fill this need.

A park surrounded by buildings in Luxembourg City

Nationality of Luxembourg Residents (2001 census)

Luxembourger	63.0%
Portuguese	13.3%
French	4.5%
Italian	4.3%
Belgian	3.4%
German	2.3%
Other	9.2%

Many immigrant workers get jobs in construction.

Many immigrants come to Luxembourg to work in the construction, manufacturing, or banking industries. As a result, Luxembourg has a higher percentage of foreign-born residents than any other country in Europe. About 37 percent of the population was born in other countries. Portuguese people are the largest foreign-born group. They make up more than one-third of the immigrant

population. Other immigrants include Italian, French, Belgian, and German nationals.

Luxembourg officials believe that the country's population could reach 700,000 by the year 2050. Many Luxembourgers think that the increase would consist mostly of immigrants. That would make native Luxembourgers a minority in their own country. The "700,000 debate" became a hot public issue in the early 2000s.

Population Trends

Today, people from many countries are moving into Luxembourg, but this has not always been the case. Throughout much of the 1800s, Luxembourg's population trend was emigration, or the movement of people out of the country. Many emigrated to the United States, while others moved to South America or other European countries. Between 1841 and 1891, about 72,000 Luxembourgers emigrated to the United States and France.

People left Luxembourg for many reasons. Farmers, laborers, and craftspeople could hardly make a living in the country. Available farmland was scarce, and farmers were plagued with famines and bad harvests. Some people left for political reasons, too. People of the lower classes paid high taxes, and only the wealthy had the right to vote.

To poverty-stricken Luxembourgers, the United States seemed like a dream. Laborers and craftspeople knew they could make a higher income there. Farmers could buy large plots of land at fairly low prices. The prospect of a better life

The registration room at Ellis Island is where many immigrants started their new lives as American citizens.

with more rights was attractive, too. With no harsh class system in place, hardworking people were often welcomed as equals. Luxembourgers could become American citizens and get the right to vote.

The outward flow of people ended with the industrial development of the late 1800s. Then foreigners began moving into Luxembourg for jobs. That trend continued throughout the 1900s. In 1900, Luxembourg's population was about 200,000. In less than one hundred years, the population doubled.

Building Communities

Luxembourgers founded many communities in the United States. Most were in Minnesota, Wisconsin, Iowa, and Illinois. Today, many of those pioneer communities proudly preserve their heritage.

Crews of carpenters and stonemasons from Luxembourg restored the Marnach House near Elba, Minnesota. Immigrants John Marnach and Nicholas Majerus had built the house in the 1850s. Building crews from Luxembourg also took down the Sunnen House in Ozaukee County, Wisconsin, and rebuilt it at Ozaukee County Pioneer Village.

The entire village of Saint Donatus, Iowa (below), is on the National Register of Historic Places. Its stone Gehlen House was built by Peter Gehlen, an immigrant from Luxembourg, in 1848. Over the years, the twenty-room house has served as a post office, grocery store, and gas station. Another team of Luxembourg builders ultimately restored the house.

Three major languages are spoken in Luxembourg—French, German, and Lëtzebuergesch, which is also called Luxembourgish, Luxembourgian, and Luxembourgeois. Officially, the government calls Luxembourgish the national language. French and German are known as administrative languages.

In Luxembourg, traffic signs appear in several languages.

Language Landmarks

Many historical events led to Luxembourg's trilingual culture. Here are some of the highlights:

963   Luxembourg is founded. As part of the Germanic Franks' empire, its language is High German.

1340   Luxembourg is divided into a French-speaking area and a German-speaking area. The common people in the German area speak a dialect that became modern Luxembourgish.

1684   Under French rule, German is largely banned. Luxembourgish remains the common, everyday language.

1804   The Code Napoleon, France's code of laws, is introduced in Luxembourg.

1839   Luxembourg is reduced to its present size, with its location in the historically German-speaking area. French, however, remains the language for government, politics, and the law.

1843   Luxembourg passes a law making French and German the languages for the education system.

1941   Under German occupation during World War II, Luxembourgers assert that their mother tongue is Luxembourgish.

1960s   Immigrants flood into Luxembourg. Most come from countries that speak Romance, or Latin-based, languages. They use French, a Romance language, to speak with Luxembourgers, because neither Luxembourgish nor German is a Romance language.

1984   Luxembourgish is officially called Luxembourg's national language.

Luxembourgers are proud of their trilingual culture. It goes along with their international outlook. But which language is used in which situations? This gets rather complicated.

Luxembourgish is the country's "mother" language, and native Luxembourgers speak it at home. Outside the home, they speak Luxembourgish among themselves in everyday

French is spoken in many Luxembourg shops.

situations. In the schools, preschool instruction is in Luxembourgish. Then it switches to German for primary school and ends up in French for the upper grades.

French is spoken in the parliament and other areas of government. It's also used in most legal proceedings. But in criminal trials, witnesses are questioned in Luxembourgish. French is also commonly heard in shops and restaurants. Road signs at the entrances to villages and towns are in both French and Luxembourgish.

German is only heard regularly in schools and during conversation between native Germans. But it's the most used language in newspapers. Many Luxembourgers also speak English—especially young people and residents of the capital city.

Luxembourgish: A Struggle to Survive

Luxembourgish is a Germanic language. It came from the same roots as modern German. But the two languages parted ways centuries ago, and Luxembourgish followed a path of its own.

Luxembourgish belongs to a language branch called Moselle Franconian. It grew out of the language of the Franks who once lived along the Moselle River. Invading Romans and another wave of Franks contributed to the language. Luxembourgish ended up with its own unique sounds and words, as well as some found in modern French and German.

For a long time, Luxembourgish was only a spoken language. It had no standard spelling or grammar rules for a written form. But the country couldn't function without a written language. That's why German and French were made national languages. It was not until 1975 that an official Luxembourgish dictionary was adopted, complete with standardized spellings. Finally, in 1984, Luxembourgish became a national language.

Groups within Luxembourg are working to promote the use of Luxembourgish in public life. The language is seen more and more in newspapers, ads, and public signs. Schools are also teaching classes in Luxembourgish. Nevertheless, many Luxembourgers are concerned that their native language may fall into the background or simply die out.

A depiction of a Franconian warrior from the ninth century

Pronouncing Luxembourgish

Letter	Pronunciation
a	but (short), father (long)
ä	let
b	ball; pet (at end of syllable)
c	key; set (before e, i, or y)
d	day
e	let (short), lay (long), action (unstressed)
é	let
ë	matter
f	fat
g	go; yet (before *eg*, *en*, *er*, and *esch*); vision (sometimes before *e* or *i*); chair (at end of word)
h	hat; silent before vowels
i	bit (short), beet (long)
j	yet or vision
k	key
l	let
m	met
n	no
o	not (short), thaw (long)
p	pan
qu	quit
r	rat (back-of-mouth trill); heard (after a vowel and before a consonant)
s	zoo; sue (at end of syllable)
t	tea
u	foot (short), fool (long)
v	fat; vat (in foreign words)
w	vat
x	fax
y	bit (short); fee with rounded lips (long); yet (sometimes before a vowel)
z	pits

Spiritual Roots

THE OVERWHELMING MAJORITY OF LUXEMBOURGERS ARE Roman Catholic. Tall spires of Catholic churches and cathedrals rise above every city and town. Many Catholic feast days are also national holidays.

Catholicism has deep historical roots in Luxembourg. Yet the constitution guarantees religious freedom to all. According to a 1979 law, the government may not collect statistics on religion. Thus there is no official government report on residents' faiths.

Opposite: **This stone church in Clervaux dates back to the seventeenth century.**

Luxembourg is home to many Catholic churches.

Major Religions

Roman Catholic	87%
Protestant, Eastern Orthodox, Jewish, Muslim, and others	13%

Some sources say that Roman Catholics make up as much as 97 percent of the population. Others report a figure of 87 percent. This is probably more realistic, considering today's large immigrant population. A variety of faiths may be found among the immigrants.

Protestants make up the largest religious minority. Most belong to Lutheran and Calvinist churches. The Muslim community includes refugees from the war-torn Montenegro Region in southeastern Europe. Luxembourg is also home to members of the Greek, Serbian, and Russian Orthodox

This mosque in Pec, Kosovo, was destroyed during the Yugoslavian Civil War.

churches. A small number of Jewish people live in Luxembourg. All these religious communities flourish alongside their Catholic neighbors.

Holidays as Holy Days

Many Catholic religious holidays are times for national festivals. Even people who are not Catholic celebrate them as colorful cultural events. Some people may simply enjoy having a day off from work! Yet each religious feast is rooted in centuries-old spirituality.

Shrove Monday and Shrove Tuesday come just before Ash Wednesday, which ushers in the somber season of Lent. Lent is a time of prayer and sacrifice to prepare for Easter. One widespread Lenten practice involves the Stations of the Cross. The Stations of the Cross is a series of fourteen events leading up to Jesus's death and burial. Most depictions of the Stations of the Cross are paintings in churches, but some are outdoor sculptures. The faithful walk from one station to the next, stopping to meditate and pray at each one.

Major Religious Holidays

Shrove Monday/Tuesday	February or March (date varies)
Easter	Usually in April (date varies)
Ascension Day	Forty days after Easter
Whit Sunday (Pentecost)	Seven weeks after Easter
Assumption Day	August 15
All Saints' Day	November 1
Christmas	December 25
Saint Stephen's Day	December 26

Saint Stephen

Easter celebrates Jesus's rising from the dead. It's a time for rejoicing after the solemn Lenten season. Ascension Day, forty days after Easter, celebrates Jesus's ascent into heaven. Whit Sunday is known as Pentecost in many other countries. It falls seven weeks after Easter. Whit Sunday commemorates the day the Holy Spirit appeared before Jesus's apostles.

All Saints' Day, on November 1, is a day to honor all Christian saints. While many saints have special feast days, this day takes in all of them. The next day is All Souls' Day. It's a time to pray for loved ones who have died and to visit their graves.

Christmas celebrates the birth of Jesus. Saint Stephen's Day comes the day after Christmas. It honors Saint Stephen, who lived in the early days of Christianity. He was put to death for his religious beliefs. Stephen is considered the first Christian martyr, a person who dies for defending his or her faith.

Leaders and Saints

Luxembourg's highest Catholic Church official is the archbishop. Reporting to him are bishops who preside in various sections of the country. On the local level are the parish priests. Most towns have one parish, or congregation. People worship in the parish church, where Masses are held.

Luxembourg also has a very old monastic tradition. Monasteries are religious communities where monks live quiet lives of prayer and study. Some monasteries are called abbeys. Both men and women can embrace the monastic life. A women's monastery is also called a convent.

Groups of monks or nuns are organized into religious orders. Each order has its own system of prayer, study, and

The Archbishop of Luxembourg (seventh from right)

Saint Willibrord

Saint Willibrord (658?–739) was born in England. He spent twelve years in Ireland, where he was ordained a priest. His superior, Saint Egbert, sent him to bring Christianity to the Frisians, a Germanic people of present-day Germany and The Netherlands.

Willibrord developed friendly relations with kings and princes as well as Catholic popes. This helped him make great strides with his missionary work. Willibrord ended up in what is now Luxembourg. He opened an abbey in Echternach in 698, thanks to a generous donation of land from the nobility. Willibrord died in Echternach, and his tomb is in the basilica of his abbey. Many cures and other miracles have been credited to him.

Donatus the Protector

Saint Donatus is honored as a protector against lightning, hailstones, and storms. Thus he is important to farmers, who appeal to him to protect their fields from devastating weather. Luxembourger pioneers in America named Saint Donatus, Iowa, after him.

work. The Benedictine, Franciscan, and Dominican orders have been active in Luxembourg for centuries. Saint Willibrord lived in Luxembourg. He was a Benedictine monk who first brought Christianity to the region.

Churches and Abbeys

Most of Luxembourg's churches and abbeys are hundreds of years old. The grandest of them all is the Cathedral of Notre Dame in Luxembourg City. But many others are the focus of great devotion. Echternach's holy sites are an example. Saint Willibrord opened Luxembourg's first abbey in Echternach in 698. His remains rest in the abbey church.

The Benedictine abbey of Saint Maurice and Saint Maur is in Clervaux. Inside is an exhibit about monastic life. Prayers and the Mass are held in the abbey. They are conducted in the ancient Gregorian chant.

The church of Saint Laurent in Diekirch was built upon the foundations of a Roman temple. Parts of the old Roman walls can still be seen there. A cemetery dating from the 500s was discovered beneath the church. The present church is more recent. It was built a mere one thousand years ago!

The Echternach abbey

The village of Troisvierges takes its name from its church. The church was once part of a convent for Franciscan nuns. It is known for its three statues—the Troisvierges, or Three Virgins—representing faith, hope, and charity.

Vianden's Church of the Trinitarians was built in 1248 for the Trinitarian religious order. Huge arches rise to the ceiling, and the altar is very ornate. Dudelange's parish church is Saint Martin of Dudelange. It's one of the largest churches in Luxembourg. The walls are covered with magnificent murals, or wall paintings.

The entrance to Notre Dame is an example of Gothic architecture.

Stained glass window depicting Mary, the mother of Jesus

Saint John's Church in Luxembourg City was built in the 1600s. It contains a picture of the Black Madonna. This image of a dark-skinned Mary is said to have worked many miracles. These are just a few of Luxembourg's historic churches and abbeys. Each one is rich in history and tradition.

Our Lady and the Octave

The elegant Cathedral of Notre Dame (Our Lady) stands in the heart of Luxembourg City. Actually, the cathedral's full name is Our Lady, Comforter of the Afflicted. This name dates from the 1600s, when the country was torn by wars, plague, and famine. A priest carried a statue of Mary, the mother of Jesus, through the streets.

In time, thousands of people joined the procession to pray for comfort. The statue was eventually placed in a chapel that is now the oldest part of the cathedral. Mary, Comforter of the Afflicted, was declared the patron saint of the city.

This procession still takes place every spring during a devotion called the Octave. The Octave began as an eight-day celebration. Now it lasts two weeks, beginning the third Sunday after Easter. At this time, devout Catholics from Luxembourg and surrounding regions make a pilgrimage, or religious journey, to the cathedral. On the last day of the Octave, the royal family leads a grand procession to the cathedral. Then a final ceremony is held in the church. Luxembourgers in Germany and the United States have continued the devotion to Our Lady of Luxembourg.

Luxembourgers participate in a procession.

Springprozession

Echternach holds a famous religious festival in honor of Saint Willibrord. Thousands of pilgrims from neighboring countries swarm in to attend. Called Springprozession, it takes place on Whit Tuesday, two days after Whit Sunday. Although it's held in the springtime, the "Spring" in Springprozession doesn't stand for the season. It's the German word for "jump," and that's exactly what happens.

Springprozession is a procession filled with music and dancing.

Springprozession is a procession through the streets of town. As musicians play a hypnotic tune over and over, people dance down the street in a sort of skipping movement, turning to the left and right. Dancers wear white shirts and dark pants or skirts. They're joined to one another by holding two ends of a handkerchief between them. The dance ends up in the abbey church, where dancers encircle the tomb of Saint Willibrord. Prayers and a devotional service end the festivities.

The celebration of Springprozession began shortly after Saint Willibrord's death. But no one has been able to make a connection between the dance and the saint himself. Some historians suggest that the dance began in pre-Christian times. In later centuries, people made the procession as a prayer for protection against the plague, epilepsy, or a nervous disorder called Saint Vitus's dance. As times changed, the celebration changed. Yet it remains a vital part of Luxembourg's religious heritage.

The Fiddling Thief

Luxembourgers enjoy a popular folk legend about the origin of Springprozession. It says that a horse thief named Veidt was condemned to death and granted one last wish before his execution in Echternach's village square. He asked for his fiddle so he could play one last time. As he struck up a lively tune, villagers could not resist dancing gaily around the square. Such delightful chaos broke out that Veidt was able to slip away unseen. Ever since, so the legend goes, the villagers of Echternach have danced on that day.

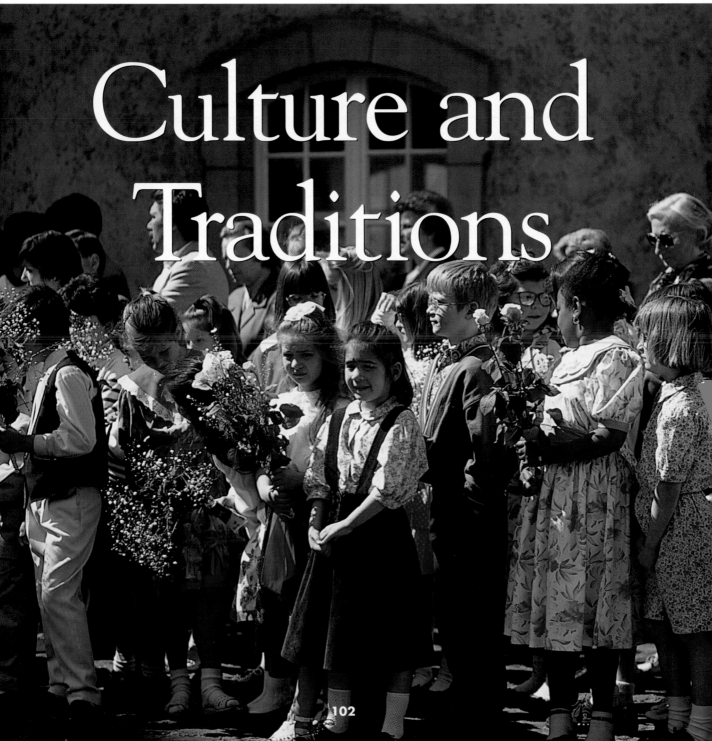

Culture and Traditions

A Carnival festival
in Echternach

Festivals are a colorful part of life in Luxembourg. The biggest national festival is Carnival. It's held just before Lent, on the days leading up to Ash Wednesday. People dress in colorful costumes and dance through the streets. They throw candies, and people catch them in upturned umbrellas.

The next Sunday is Buurgbrennen (Bonfire Day), when fires are lit on the hillsides at night. This feast remains from pre-Christian times. In those days, the fires symbolized the sun's victory over winter.

May 1 is May Day. People in villages and towns go into the forest and collect the first green branches that have sprouted.

Opposite: **Children gather for the Har Leichens procession.**

The Grand Duke and Duchess
of Luxembourg attend Mass
on National Day.

They weave them into a Meekranz, or May wreath, as a symbol of nature's rebirth. Back in the village, a band leads a joyful procession, and the wreaths are hung outside churches and taverns.

On the eve of National Day (June 23), Luxembourg City holds a torchlight parade and fireworks. The next day, the royal family goes to the cathedral for a Te Deum—a solemn Mass in honor of the grand duke. Parties and merrymaking fill the rest of the day.

Schueberfouer is a two-week fun fair in Luxembourg City, with rides, food stalls, and music. It takes place in late August and early September. It has been held for more than six hundred years, commemorating a shepherd's fair founded by Saint John the Blind in 1340. A highlight of the fair is the Hämmelsmarsch, or sheep march, when sheep decorated with colorful ribbons parade through the streets. The final day is a national holiday. The day ends with a big fireworks display.

In the autumn, many wine festivals take place in the Moselle Valley. They end with Wormeldange's New Wine Festival. Vianden holds its Nut Market in October. Walnuts are a local product, and townspeople celebrate with walnut candy, walnut cakes, and even walnut pizza. The high point is—what else?—the walnut parade!

Pretzel Sunday

Bratzelsonndeg, or Pretzel Sunday, is the fourth Sunday of Lent. Boys give a pretzel to their girlfriends that day. On Easter, girls give their boyfriends painted eggs in return. The stronger the sweetheart's feelings are, the bigger and more ornate the gift is. In leap years, things are switched around. Then girls give pretzels and boys give eggs.

Éimaischen

Easter Monday is the day for *Éimaischen* in the town of Nospelt. It's a time for street parties, flea markets, and a charming local tradition.

Nospelt began as a pottery village. At the end of their workday, the potters used to sculpt their leftover clay into *peckvillchen*—whistles shaped like birds. Now on Éimaischen, sweethearts exchange the little birds as a token of their love.

December Festivities

Much excitement leads up to the feast of Saint Nicholas on December 6. In Luxembourg, the jolly, bearded Saint Nick is called Kleeschen. He can be seen in all the shops, where children sit on his lap. He asks them if they've been good, and they tell him what presents they want.

Beginning on December 1, children put their shoes outside their bedroom doors and find treats inside them in the morning. Then, on the night of December 5, Kleeschen comes and brings gifts while everyone is asleep. But children are not to take this for granted. Houseker, or Black Peter, roams around that same night, all dressed in black. He carries sticks for spanking naughty children!

Poinsettias decorate the windowsills during the Christmas season. On Christmas Eve, people gather around the Christmas tree, exchange gifts, and share a hearty meal. Many people also attend midnight church

Saint Nicholas

services. This time, it's Chrëschtkëndchen—the Christ Child—who brings gifts to children during the night. Christmas Day is a time for a big dinner with family and friends. They wish one another the season's greetings—*"Schéi Chrëschtdeeg!"* It's the Luxembourgish version of "Merry Christmas!"

Poinsettias are a common Christmas decoration in Luxembourg.

New Year's Eve calls for a special family meal. Many people go out to dance at festive balls. Then, at midnight, everyone pours into the streets to watch a glorious fireworks display.

Annual Public Holidays

New Year's Day	January 1
Carnival	Monday before Lent begins (date varies)
Easter Monday	Day after Easter (date varies)
Labor Day	May 1
Ascension Day	Forty days after Easter
Whit Monday	Day after Whit Sunday
National Day	June 23
Assumption Day	August 15
Schueberfouer	First Monday in September (Luxembourg City only)
All Saints' Day	November 1
Christmas	December 25
Saint Stephen's Day	December 26

The Music Conservatory in Luxembourg hosts many concerts.

Music Across the Land

Music is part of almost every celebration in Luxembourg. Even the smallest towns and villages have their own bands and singing groups. When it's time for a parade, people march along to the tunes of their local band.

Echternach holds its International Music Festival every summer. Solo musicians and music groups come from around the world. Most concerts and recitals are held in the basilica where Saint Willibrord is buried. Many other cities and towns hold music events throughout the year. The town of Wiltz hosts an international music and theater festival every July.

Luxembourg City is home to the Luxembourg Philharmonic Orchestra. It offers weekly evening concerts, as well as noon concerts in the main city park. The city also has a spring music festival and Summer in the City concerts. At the end of the summer, Luxembourg holds a competition for musicians throughout the country.

I. M. Pei

For Art Lovers

Luxembourg's finest art museums are in the capital city. The National Museum of History and Art displays art and artifacts from centuries of history. Architect I. M. Pei designed the

Art of Many Ages

The National Museum of History and Art in Luxembourg City is the country's finest cultural museum. It displays art and objects from pre-Roman times through the twentieth century. The exhibits explore the country's history, art, daily life, and folklore.

Among the museum's holdings are archaeological objects, paintings, weapons, coins, and documents. The archaeological collections are displayed in exhibit areas that have been carved out of rock. The Luxembourg Life exhibits are spread across four residences. They are decorated like typical Luxembourgers' homes in past centuries.

beautiful Grand Duke Jean Museum of Modern Art. It opened in 2005 and stands among the many modern buildings and sculptures on the city's Kirchberg Plateau.

Joseph Kutter (1894–1941) is respected as Luxembourg's greatest artist. He introduced Luxembourgers to modern art. Kutter painted in an expressionist style. This style expresses strong emotion, rather than just depicting an object or scene.

Luxembourgers are also proud of photographer Edward Steichen. He was born in Luxembourg, although he spent his career in the United States. Works by both Kutter and Steichen are shown in Luxembourg's museums and galleries.

A photo taken by Edward Steichen of fighter planes over Florida

Photography Pioneer

Edward Steichen (1879–1973) was a pioneer in the early days of photography. He was born in the village of Bivange, Luxembourg. When he was three years old, he and his family moved to Michigan. He began experimenting with color photography in 1904, long before most other photographers. During World War I (1914–1918), he worked as an aerial photographer. Later, he worked as a commercial photographer and also photographed many famous actors and writers.

Steichen became director of photography at the Museum of Modern Art in New York City. In 1955, he assembled the *Family of Man* exhibit there. With more than five hundred photographs from sixty-eight countries, it was one of the most popular photography shows of all time. The exhibit now has a permanent home in Luxembourg's Clervaux castle.

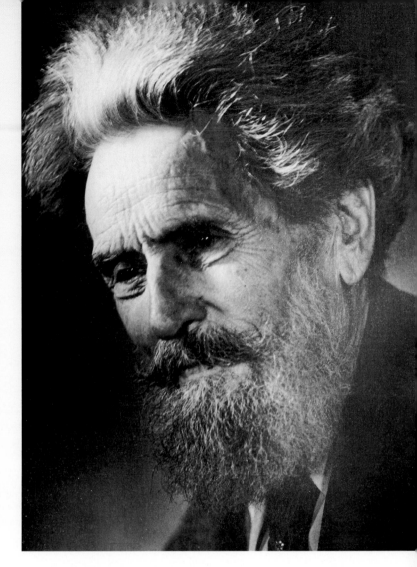

Literature

Luxembourger authors have had the choice of writing in German, French, or Luxembourgish. It was only in the 1800s that the Luxembourgish language began to appear in literature.

Edmond de la Fontaine (1823–1891) went by the name of Dicks. He wrote poetry, plays, and songs in Luxembourgish.

Fox Tales

Michel Rodange's *De Renert* tells fourteen tales about a wily fox. Renert has committed many terrible deeds. The worst of them is murdering a hen. Many times, he is brought before the king to receive his punishment. Just as many times, he manages to talk his way to freedom.

In one episode, Renert weeps before the king, saying he is the victim of his evil accusers. Moved by Renert's appeal, the king frees him and imprisons the accusers instead. In another scene, Renert tells the king he'll fight a duel with the wolf, one of his accusers. Renert wins through a dirty trick and humbly returns to face the king. At last, the king forgives Renert. He makes the fox his minister, and all the other animals must bow down to him.

Of course, these outcomes are clearly not fair. Rodange used the tales to criticize and make fun of Luxembourg's political conditions at the time.

Many of his songs are still popular in Luxembourg. Dicks collected proverbs and other folklore from around the countryside. These touches of folklife enriched his writings.

Michel Rodange (1827–1876) wrote the epic poem *De Renert*. It's a Luxembourgian version of a traditional German tale about a fox. Rodange's tricky, dishonest fox reflects the political and cultural turmoil of the time. A statue of Renert the fox, who always wears a suit, sits atop a monument to Rodange in Luxembourg City.

Michel Lentz (1820–1893) wrote the poem "Ons Héemécht" ("Our Homeland"), which became Luxembourg's national anthem. Lentz wrote many other poems for formal and festive occasions. He wanted his works to celebrate Luxembourg's national pride.

In the twentieth century, many more writers began using the Luxembourgish language. One of the best-known modern writers is Roger Manderscheid. He writes in both German and

Luxembourgish, producing novels, short stories, poetry, dramas, and radio plays.

Guy Renewig has written several novels in Luxembourgish since it became an official language in 1984. His children's book *Komba la Bomba* is about a girl from the Cape Verde Islands who wants to be a soccer star in Luxembourg. Jhemp Hoscheit is a very popular children's book author who writes in Luxembourgish.

On the Silver Screen

The movies *American Werewolf in Paris* (1997) and *Shadow of the Vampire* (2000) (below) were filmed in Luxembourg. The country's castles, with their dark chambers and tunnels, make great movie sets!

Just about everyone in Luxembourg can read and write. The country's education system is tough, but it produces very well-educated citizens. Most students end up trilingual, speaking all three of Luxembourg's official languages.

At age four, children begin preschool, which is taught in the Luxembourgish language. Two years of preschool are

Children in Luxembourg first learn Luxembourgish.

required by law. Primary school lasts six years, from age six through twelve. Classes are in German, but French is introduced in the second grade. After age twelve, a student can continue with either secondary school or technical school. Secondary school lasts seven years. By the upper years of secondary school, French is the language of instruction. Technical school can last six to eight years.

The University of Luxembourg

Luxembourg City's University Center offers courses in many subjects. Students then go on to a university outside the country, as Luxembourg has only just begun to develop its own university. For technical students, the Institut Supérieur de Technologies offers higher education in computer science, electrical engineering, and other technical fields.

Building a Future on the Past

It's been said that Luxembourgers live with one foot in the past and the other in the future. Nowhere is this more obvious than in Luxembourg City. Its ultra-modern European Center looks like a vision of the future. Here, people in business clothes are hard at work every day. They're tending to serious matters of finance and international affairs. In many ways, the future of Europe rests in their hands.

From their gleaming office buildings, these workers can look down to the old city center. They see ancient fortifications and medieval church towers. In these surroundings, the

Opposite: **Old Luxembourg City**

The Luxembourg financial district

pace of life is much more leisurely. People are strolling through the streets and open squares. They're browsing through museums, shopping, and enjoying outdoor cafés. Artists are sketching portraits, and merchants are selling fruits and vegetables. Joggers run through wooded parks with beautiful views overlooking the river.

A woman shops for flowers at an outdoor market.

Living Spaces

When it comes to housing, the future is quickly pushing the past aside. As Luxembourg City's businesses grow, more and more people need places to live. Many houses and apartments in the city were built decades or even centuries ago. People who want newer homes often go to the surrounding suburbs. Suburban housing developments are going up as fast as workers can build them.

Out in the countryside, many villages still have cobblestone streets. Shops crowd the village square, and market day brings out the open-air stalls. Stone structures are everywhere. Houses and barns are built of stone. So are garden fences, grave markers, and wayside crosses. Some stone houses are coated with earth-colored stucco, while others may be whitewashed.

Many people live in homes that have been in the family for generations. Still, modern life has reached these places, too. A supermarket or gas station may stand next to buildings that are hundreds of years old.

Hillside houses in Montee De La Petrusse

All-Purpose Homes

In the 1800s, the *Quereinhaus* was a typical home. It was a long, rectangular building that combined a house, stable, and barn under one roof. Grain and fruits were stored on the second floor.

Luxembourgers have a passion for soccer.

Sports and Recreation

Like the rest of Europe, Luxembourg is wild about football—which means soccer. The national soccer team competes in the Union of European Football Associations (UEFA). It's always exciting when Luxembourg makes it to the European Championships. Luxembourg reached the quarter-finals once, in 1963, and loyal fans keep hoping for a better showing.

Angel of the Mountains

Luxembourg's Charly Gaul (1932–) became a national hero when he won the Tour de France bicycle race in 1958. Charly's nickname was the Angel of the Mountains. He'd whiz past his opponents on uphill climbs. His finest feat in the 1958 race was finishing the last big climbing stage more than eight minutes ahead of the next racer. Charly's secret for climbing was to use the lowest gear and pedal as fast as possible.

Bicycling is a popular sport, both to do and to watch. Locals and tourists alike enjoy bike tours through the countryside. They can follow the *Radwanderwege*, or protected bike paths, all through the country. Luxembourg holds an annual bike race called the Tour du Luxembourg. It's a smaller version of the famous Tour de France race. The streets were packed with onlookers in 2002, when the Tour de France set off from Luxembourg City.

Luxembourg's lakes and rivers are great for swimming, canoeing, waterskiing, windsurfing, and sailing. Some

The 2002 Tour de France

people head to the Ardennes for mountain climbing and rock climbing. Others simply enjoy the scenery by walking or hiking along the forest trails. Hundreds of miles of hiking paths wind through Luxembourg's forests, fields, and villages. A hardy hiker can cross the country from east to west in just one day!

Cross-country skiing is a favorite winter sport in the Ardennes. The slopes are not long and steep enough for downhill skiing, though. Once the lakes and rivers freeze over, they're perfect for ice skating. Luxembourg City has an outdoor ice-skating rink at Place Guillaume. Other popular sports

Trails through Luxembourg's woods offer beautiful scenery.

D'Coque

Luxembourg City's gigantic National Sports and Cultural Center opened in 2002. Called d'Coque for short, this massive complex is one of the several modern structures on the Kirchberg Plateau. There are many different spaces under the three curved domes of its roof. An eight-thousand-seat arena holds sports events, concerts, and other shows. In the training center, athletes can work out at martial arts, weightlifting, boxing, and other sports. The one-thousand-seat gymnasium showcases a number of sporting events and exhibitions. The aquatic center includes two Olympic-size swimming pools. A restaurant, conference center, and hotel rooms round out the complex.

are basketball, volleyball, table tennis, and squash (a kind of racquetball game).

Ice skating is a favorite winter pastime in Luxembourg.

The Fairy-Tale Park

Thousands of visitors come to Bettembourg's Parc Merveilleux every year. It's a children's park full of fairy-tale scenes and exhibits, exotic animals, mini-cars, a miniature train, and playgrounds.

Hearty Eating

Food in Luxembourg is hearty and often heavy. It's served in generous portions, and a dinner guest is expected to have seconds. Most traditional dishes originated among the peasants, who concocted them from their farm products.

Hearty dishes featuring meat are popular in Luxembourg.

Sausages in a market stall

Pork meat and other pig parts show up in many dishes. The national dish is *Judd mat Gaardebounen*—smoked pork neck with broad beans in a thick, creamy sauce. *Träipen* are black-pudding sausages made of pigs' organs and vegetables. It's easy to see the farm connection with *Ham am Hee*. It's ham cooked in hay!

Traditional soups include *Bouneschlupp* (green bean soup) and *Gromperenzopp* (potato soup). *Gromperekichelcher* are deep-fried potato pancakes with onions and parsley. Cheese, sausages, and sauerkraut are often served as side dishes.

Luxembourg's freshly baked bread is great for sopping up juices. It's also eaten with spreads such as *Kachkéis* (a cooked cheese) or *Pati* (a meat spread). For dessert, there are fruit tarts such as *Quetscheflued* (plum tart). Moselle wines and local beers are popular drinks. When people drink water with a meal, they usually drink bottled mineral water.

Holidays call for special foods. Gingerbread men (*Boxemännercher*) are a favorite children's treat on Saint Nicholas Day. The Christmas season brings out fruit-filled

Gingerbread men are a Christmas treat.

Making *Gromperekichelcher* (Potato Pancakes)

Potato pancakes served with applesauce are a favorite winter treat in Luxembourg.

Ingredients:

2 pounds potatoes

2 medium onions

2 shallots

Several sprigs parsley

4–6 eggs

Salt

Pepper

$\frac{1}{4} - \frac{1}{2}$ cup vegetable oil

2 tablespoons flour

Applesauce

Directions:

Wash, peel, and grate the potatoes. Lay them on a dishcloth or paper towel, fold it over, and press the moisture out. Put the grated potatoes into a mixing bowl. Chop the onions, shallots, and parsley, and mix with the potatoes. Beat the eggs and mix them in. Add salt and pepper to suit your taste.

Heat the oil in a frying pan until it's very hot. Meanwhile, spread the flour onto a smooth surface for working with the potatoes. Shape the potato mixture into balls and mash them to make flat cakes. Fry the potato cakes in the oil, turning once so they're golden brown on both sides. Serve with applesauce on top or on the side.

pancakes called crêpes and tasty little Thüringer sausages. For dinner on Christmas Day, there's black pudding with mashed potatoes and applesauce. The traditional Christmas dessert is stollen. It's a fruit-filled cake baked in the shape of a log. New Year's Eve calls for *raclette*, which is boiled potatoes with melted Swiss cheese.

Whether they're working, playing, or eating, Luxembourgers are proud of their rich heritage. It's easy to see why they say, "We want to stay as we are!"

Crêpes are a popular Luxembourg pastry.

Building a Future on the Past   **127**

Timeline

Luxembourg History

Celtic people live in present-day Luxembourg.	*ca.* 700 B.C.
The Treveri people live in Luxembourg.	*ca.* 400s B.C.
Julius Caesar conquers the Luxembourg Region. Luxembourg becomes part of the Roman Empire.	53 B.C.
The Franks take over a vast region that includes Luxembourg.	A.D. 400s
Saint Willibrord establishes Luxembourg's first abbey at Echternach.	698
Siegfried, count of Ardennes, establishes Luxembourg as an independent state.	963
Henry VII, count of Luxembourg, becomes Holy Roman Emperor.	1308
John the Blind holds a shepherd's fair that survives today as Luxembourg City's Schueberfouer festival.	1340
Charles IV creates the duchy of Luxembourg.	1354
Luxembourg's independence ends when Burgundy takes it over.	1443
One European power after another rules Luxembourg.	1477–1815

World History

2500 B.C.	Egyptians build the Pyramids and the Sphinx in Giza.
563 B.C.	The Buddha is born in India.
A.D. 313	The Roman emperor Constantine recognizes Christianity.
610	The Prophet Muhammad begins preaching a new religion called Islam.
1054	The Eastern (Orthodox) and Western (Roman) Churches break apart.
1066	William the Conqueror defeats the English in the Battle of Hastings.
1095	Pope Urban II proclaims the First Crusade.
1215	King John seals the Magna Carta.
1300s	The Renaissance begins in Italy.
1347	The Black Death sweeps through Europe.
1453	Ottoman Turks capture Constantinople, conquering the Byzantine Empire.
1492	Columbus arrives in North America.
1500s	The Reformation leads to the birth of Protestantism.
1776	The Declaration of Independence is signed.
1789	The French Revolution begins.

Luxembourg History

The Congress of Vienna creates the Grand Duchy of Luxembourg, a possession of The Netherlands.	1815
Luxembourg is partitioned, with most of the territory going to Belgium.	1839
Luxembourg achieves full independence.	1867
Grand Duke Adolf begins Luxembourg's hereditary dynasty of the House of Nassau.	1890
Germany occupies Luxembourg during World War I.	1914–1918
Grand Duchess Charlotte becomes Luxembourg's monarch.	1919
Germany occupies Luxembourg during World War II.	1940–1944
The monthlong Battle of the Bulge takes place in the Ardennes forest.	1944–1945
Luxembourg helps form the United Nations.	1945
Luxembourg joins the North Atlantic Treaty Organization.	1949
Luxembourg is one of the six founding nations of the European Economic Community.	1957
Luxembourg's Charly Gaul wins the Tour de France bicycle race.	1958
Grand Duchess Charlotte steps down, and her son Jean becomes grand duke.	1964
Luxembourgish becomes a national language.	1984
Luxembourg helps found the European Union.	1993
Jean-Claude Juncker becomes prime minister.	1995
Grand Duke Henri assumes the throne as his father, Grand Duke Jean, steps down.	2000
Luxembourg begins using the euro as its currency.	2002

World History

1865	The American Civil War ends.
1914	World War I breaks out.
1917	The Bolshevik Revolution brings communism to Russia.
1929	Worldwide economic depression begins.
1939	World War II begins, following the German invasion of Poland.
1945	World War II ends.
1957	The Vietnam War starts.
1969	Humans land on the moon.
1975	The Vietnam War ends.
1979	Soviet Union invades Afghanistan.
1983	Drought and famine in Africa.
1989	The Berlin Wall is torn down, as communism crumbles in Eastern Europe.
1991	Soviet Union breaks into separate states.
1992	Bill Clinton is elected U.S. president.
2000	George W. Bush is elected U.S. president.
2001	Terrorists attack World Trade Towers, New York and the Pentagon, Washington, D.C.

Fast Facts

Official name: Grand Duchy of Luxembourg

Capital: Luxembourg City

Official languages: French, German, and Luxembourgish

A few of Luxembourg City's many historic buildings

Luxembourg's flag

Insenborn

Year of founding:	963
Founder:	Siegfried, count of Ardennes
National anthem:	*"Ons Héemécht"* ("Our Homeland"); words by Michel Lentz, music by Jean-Antoine Zinnen; adopted in 1895
Government:	Constitutional monarchy
Head of state:	Grand duke or grand duchess
Head of government:	Prime minister
Area:	999 square miles (2,586 square km)
Borders:	Belgium to the north and west, Germany to the east, France to the south
Highest elevation:	Buurgplaatz, 1,835 feet (559 m) above sea level
Lowest elevation:	435 feet (133 m) above sea level
Average temperature:	33°F (0.8°C) in January; 63.5°F (17.5°C) in July (Luxembourg City)
Average annual precipitation:	31 inches (79 cm)
Greatest distance, north–south:	55 miles (89 km)
Greatest distance, east–west:	35 miles (56 km)
Major rivers:	Moselle, Sûre, Our, and Alzette
Largest lake:	Lake of the Upper Sûre

The Bock casements

National population (2004 est.): 462,690

Population of largest cities (2004 est):

Luxembourg City	77,325
Esch-sur-Alzette	27,891
Differdange	18,891
Dudelange	17,514
Pétange	14,382

Famous landmarks:

- ▶ *Bock casemates*, Luxembourg City
- ▶ *Notre Dame Cathedral*, Luxembourg City
- ▶ *Grand Ducal Palace*, Luxembourg City
- ▶ *Bourscheid Castle*, Bourscheid
- ▶ *Clervaux Castle*, Clervaux
- ▶ *Vianden Castle*, Vianden
- ▶ *Echternach Basilica*, Echternach

Industry: Banking is Luxembourg's leading industry. More than 180 financial institutions are headquartered there. Manufactured goods include steel and other metals, food and beverages, and rubber and plastic goods. The major farm products include beef and pork, barley, wheat, potatoes, and wine grapes.

Currency: The euro is the basic unit of currency. In April 2005, 1 euro was equal to US$1.30, and US$1.00 was equal to 0.769 euros.

System of weights and measures: Metric system

Literacy rate: About 100 percent

Various examples of the euro

A teacher and his student in Luxembourg

Common words and phrases:

Luxembourgish	French	German	English
Moïen (MOY-en)	*Bonjour* (bohn-ZHOOR)	*Guten Tag* (GOOT-en TAHK)	Hello
Wéi geet et? (veh geht et)	*Comment allez-vous?* (KOH-mohnt ahl-ay-VOO)	*Wie geht es Ihnen?* (vee gayt es EE-nehn)	How are you?
Gutt (goot)	*Bien* (bee-EHN)	*Sehr gut* (zehr goot)	(I am) fine.
Äddi (EHD-dee)	*Au revoir* (OH ruh-VWAH)	*Auf Wiedersehen* (owf VEE-der-zay-ehn)	Goodbye

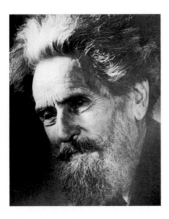

Edward Steichen

Famous Luxembourg people:

Charles IV (1316–1378)
King of Bohemia and Holy Roman Emperor

Grand Duchess Charlotte (1896–1985)
Luxembourg's monarch (1919–1964)

Grand Duke Henri (1955–)
Luxembourg's monarch (2000–)

Grand Duke Jean (1921–)
Luxembourg's monarch (1964–2000)

John the Blind (1296–1346)
Count of Luxembourg and Holy Roman Emperor

Jean-Claude Juncker (1954–)
Prime minister (1995–)

Joseph Kutter (1894–1941)
Expressionist painter

Robert Schuman (1886–1963)
Founding father of the European Union

Siegfried (ca. 918–998)
Count of Ardennes, founder of Luxembourg

Edward Steichen (1879–1973)
Pioneer photographer; best known for "Family of Man" exhibit

Saint Willibrord (ca. 658–739)
Founder of Echternach abbey

To Find Out More

Books

▶ Carrick, Noel. *Let's Visit Luxembourg*. Philadelphia: Chelsea House, 1992.

▶ McNeese, Tim. *Battle of the Bulge*. Philadelphia: Chelsea House, 2004.

▶ Petra Press. *European Union*. Milwaukee: World Almanac, 2004.

▶ Powell, Jillian. *The European Union*. Danbury, Conn: Franklin Watts, 2001.

▶ Sheehan, Patricia. *Luxembourg*. New York: Marshall Cavendish, 1999.

Videotapes

▶ *Discovering Holland, Luxembourg, Belgium*. 75 minutes. Video Visits, 1992.

▶ *The Low Countries: Holland, Belgium, and Luxembourg*. 52 minutes. Questar, Inc., 1997.

▶ *Royal Families of the World*. 115 minutes. Goldhil Home Media, 1999.

Web Sites

▶ **Luxembourg Central**
http://www.luxcentral.com/
index/shtml
*A survey of Luxembourg's language,
traditions, holidays, and foods.*

Luxembourg Tourist Office
▶ http://www.luxembourg.co.uk/
*An extensive look at Luxembourg's
culture, history, and points of interest.*

▶ **Touring Luxembourg**
http://www.awcluxembourg.com/
webpages/lil_update/travel.htm
*A guide to Luxembourg's cities, towns,
and historic sites.*

Embassy

▶ **Embassy of the Grand Duchy of
Luxembourg**
2200 Massachusetts Avenue NW
Washington, D.C. 20008
(202) 265-4171
www.luxembourg-usa.org/

Index

Page numbers in *italics* indicate illustrations.

352 newspaper, 75

A

Administrative Court, 58
administrative languages, 84
Adolf (grand duke), 47
agriculture
    Bon Pays region, 20
    Donatus (saint) and, 96
    emigration and, 81
    livestock, 20, 68, *68*
    Moselle Valley, 27
    Oesling region, 20
    vineyards, 11, 21, 27, *27*, 69, *69*
    wild boars and, 32
All Saints' Day, 94
Alzette River, 18, 25, 42
Alzette Valley, *16*
American Military Cemetery, 49
American Werewolf in Paris (film), 113
animal life
    Ardennes region, 32–33
    badgers, *34*, 34
    birds, 34, *34*, 35, *35*, 36, *36*
    crested grebes, 35, *35*
    endangered, 33–34
    golden orioles, 36, *36*
    Haff Réimech wetland, 35, *35*
    hares, 33, *33*
    little stonechats, 36
    livestock, 20, 68, *68*
    pheasants, 34, *34*

    polecats, 33–34
    wild boars, 32, *32*
Ansembourg Castle, 45, *45*
Arcelor company, 66
Ardennes region, 11, 19–20, *19*, 22, 26, 27, 30, 32, 49, 122
art, 109–111
artesian maze caves, 24
Ascension Day, 94
Ash Wednesday, 93, 103
ASTRA satellites, 75
Austrasia kingdom, 40

B

badgers, 34, *34*
Battle of Crécy, 43
Battle of the Bulge, 23, 48–49, *48*, *49*
Belgica province, 39
Belgium, 17
Benedictine abbey, 22
Benedictine order, 96
Benelux countries, 18
Benelux Economic Union, 18
Bessemer process, 65
bicycling, 121, *121*
Bilzen, *10*
birds, 34, *34*, 35, *35*, 36, *36*
Black Ernz valley, 24
Bock Rock, 25, *38*, *41*, 60
Bon Pays region, 20–21, 68
borders, 17, 21, 37, 50–51
Bouillon, *17*

Bourscheid Castle, 22
Bratzelsonndeg, 105
Broom Flower Festival, 30
broom flowers, 31, *31*
Butterfly Garden, 33
Buurgbrennen, 103
Buurgplaatz hill, 18, 19

C

Caesar, Julius, 10, 29, 39
Calvinists, 92
Cargolux airline, 71
Carnival, 103, *103*
caverns, 24
caves, 24
Celtic tribes, 10, 39
Cercle Municipal, *59*
Chamber of Deputies, 55
Charlemagne (Frankish king), 40
Charles IV, king of Bohemia,
    42–43, *42*, 133
Charlotte (grand duchess), 47, 53,
    53, 54, 133
Chateau De Beafort, *8*
Chemin de la Corniche, 60
Christmas, 94, 106–107, 126–127
Church of Saint Laurent, 23
Church of the Trinitarians, 98
cities. *See also* Luxembourg City;
    towns; villages.
    Differdange, 46, 78, 79
    Dudelange, 46, 78, 79, 98
    Esch-sur-Alzette, 20, *20*, 23, 46,
        78, 79
    Esch-sur-Sûre, 22, 23, *29*, 37
    Grevenmacher, 33
    Pétange, 46, 78, 79
    Trier, 39
Clervaux castle, 12, 19, 22, *90*,
    97, 111
climate, 18, 26–27, 61

Code Napoleon, 85
communications, 14, 74–75, *74*
Congress of Vienna, 44
constitution, 53, 91
Constitutional Court, 58
convents, 95
Coolidge, Elizabeth, *67*
d'Coque complex, 123
Council of Ministers, 51, 56
Council of State, 54
crested grebes, 35, *35*
cross-country skiing, 122
currency (euro), 64, *64*

D

De Renert (Michel Rodange), 112
deciduous trees, 30
Deiwelselter monument, 39
Department of Forests, 29
Diekirch, 23, 39, 97
Differdange, 46, 78, 79
district courts, 58
Dolle, Guy, *66*
dolmen (monument), 39
Dominican order, 96
Donatus (saint), 96
Dudelange, 46, 78, 79, 98
Durbuy, *26*

E

Easter, 93, 94
Echternach, 23, *23*, 100, *103*, 108
Echternach abbey, 96, *97*
economy
    agriculture, 68–69
    banking industry, *62*, 63–65
    cross-border workers, 69–70
    European Economic Community
        (EEC), 51
    gross domestic product (GDP), 63
    high-tech industries, 70–71

household spending, 70
international business, 14
manufacturing, 65–66, 68
mining, 20, 65, 68
national income, 63
service jobs, 63
steel industry, 65
education, 9–10, *9*, 48, 86, 88,
    114–115
Edward III, king of England, 43
Egbert (saint), 96
Ehnen village, *21*
Éimaischen, 106
Eisch River valley, 45
endangered animals, 33–34
English language, 74, 75, 87
Esch-sur-Alzette, 20, *20*, 23, 46,
    78, 79
Esch-sur-Sûre, 22, 23, *29*, 37
euro (currency), 64, *64*
European Coal and Steel Community.
    (ECSC), 50, 51
European Court of Justice, 51, *58*, 61
European Economic Community
    (EEC), 51
European Union (EU), 14, 50, 51
evergreen trees, 30, *30*
executive branch of government,
    55–57

F

festivals, 103, *103*
Findel Airport, *71*
Fontainte, Edmond de la, 111–112
food, 124–127, *124*, *125*, *126*, *127*
Forest of the Ardennes, 29
Franciscan order, 96
Frankish tribes, 10–11, 40, 85, 87, *88*
French language, 9, 14, 45, 48, 74,
    75, 84, 85, 86, *86*, 87, 111, 115
Frisian people, 96

G

Gaul, Charly, 121, *121*
Gaul region, 39
Gehlen House, 83
Gehlen, Peter, 83
geography
    Ardennes region, 11, 19–20, *19*, 22,
        26, 27, 30, 32, 49, 122
    Bon Pays region, 20–21, 68
    borders, 17
    Buurgplaatz hill, 19
    caverns, 24
    caves, 24
    elevation, 18
    land area, 17, 18
    Low Countries, 18
    Moselle Valley, 11, 21, *21*, 27, 105
    Müllerthal region, 21, 23, 24, 27
    waterways, 24–26
geopolitical map, *11*
German language, 9, 14, 40, 74, 75, 84,
    85, 86, 87, 111, 115
Germanic tribes, 10
Germano-Luxembourg Nature Park, 37
Germany, 47–48, 48–49
golden orioles, 36, *36*
government
    Chamber of Deputies, 55
    constitutional monarchy, 53
    Council of State, 54, 55
    elections, 55
    European Union (EU), 14
    executive branch, 55
    grand duchy, 53–54, 55–56
    House of Nassau, 53
    judicial branch, 55, 57–58
    legislative branch, 55
    local, 59
    neutrality, 46
    Parliament, 55, *55*, 56, 57, 87
    political parties, 57
    prime ministers, 56–57
    regional, 59
Grand Ducal Palace, *52*, 60
Grand Duke Jean Museum of Modern
    Art, 110
"The Great 208" radio station, 74
Greek Orthodox Church, 92–93
Green Heart of Europe, 11, 29
Grevenmacher, 33
gromperekichelcher (potato pancakes),
    127
gross domestic product (GDP), 63
Grotte Sainte-Barbe, 24
Grünwald forest, 31
Gutland region. *See* Bon Pays region.

H

Haff Réimech wetland, 35, *35*
Hamm, 49
Hämmelsmarsch, 105
Hapsburg dynasty, 44
Har Lichens procession, *102*
hares, 33, *33*
Henri (grand duke), 53, 54, *54*, 133
Henry VII (emperor), 42
historical maps. *See also* maps.
    Battle of the Bulge, *49*
    Divided Luxembourg, *44*
    Early Luxembourg, *40*
holidays
    national, 54, *54*, 107
    religious, 93–94
Hollenfels castle, 45
House of Nassau, 47, 53
Hugo, Victor, 22

I

insect life, 33
Insenborn, *28*
Institut Supérieur de Technologies, 115
International Music Festival, 108

J

Jean (grand duke), 53, 54, *54*, 133
John the Blind, king of Bohemia, 42, 43, *43*, 105, 133
Judaism, 93
judicial branch of government, 55, 57–58
Juncker, Jean-Claude, 57, *57*, 133

K

Kadenauer Building, *55*
Keltenheil cave, 24
Kirchberg Plateau, 61, 123
Kleeschen (Saint Nick), 106, *106*
Koerich castle, 45
Komba la Bomba (Guy Renewig), 113
Kroll Process, 67
Kroll, William J., 67, *67*
Kutter, Joseph, 110

L

Lake of the Upper Sûre, 18, 22, 26, 37
Land of the Red Earth, 20
languages, 9–10, 40, 84–87, *84*, 114
Latin language, 40
legislative branch of government, 55
Lent, 93, 103
Lentz, Michel, 112
Lëtzebuerger Journal newspaper, 75
literature, 111–113
little stonechats (bird), 36
livestock, 68, *68*
local government, 59
Low Countries, 18
Lucilinburhuc, 41
Lutherans, 92
Luxair airline, 71
The Luxembourg News newspaper, 75

Luxembourg City, 20, 25, 31, 32, 41, *41*, 43, 49, 50, 51, 60–61, *60*, *61*, 71, 72, 78, 79, *79*, 96, 99, 105, 108, 109, 115, 117, 118, 121, 122
Luxembourg City Historical Museum, 60
Luxembourg Philharmonic Orchestra, 108
Luxembourgish language, 9, 14, 45, 48, 84, 85–86, 87–89, 111, 114

M

Maastricht Treaty, 51
Majerus, Nicholas, 83
Manderscheid, Roger, 112–113
manufacturing, 68
maps. *See also* historical maps.
    geopolitical, *11*
    Luxembourg City, *61*
    natural resources, *69*
    population density, *79*
    topographical, *18*
Maria Térèsa (grand duchess), 54
Marnach, John, 83
May Day, 103, 105
Melusina, 42
Mersch castle, 45
Mertert, 73
metric system, 65
Middle Stone Age, 39
mining, 20, 23, 46, 65, 68
Moestroff Cave, 24
monasteries, 95
Montee de la Petrusse Hillside House, *119*
Moselle Franconian language branch, 87
Moselle Nature Park, 37
Moselle River, 18, 24, 25, 39, 73

Moselle Valley, 11, 21, *21*, 27, 105
Moselle wine, 69
Müllerthal region, 21, 23, 24, 27
Museum of Dolls and Toys, 22
Museum of Roman Mosaics, 23
Museum of Rustic Arts, 22
Museum of the National Resistance, 23
music, 108, *108*
Muslims, 92

N

national anthem, 56, 112
National Day, 54, *54*, *104*, 105
national dish, 125
national flag, *46*, 56, *56*
national holidays, 107, 126–127
national language, 84, 85
national motto, 77
National Museum of History and Art, 109
National Museum of Military History, 23
National Museum of Natural History, 32
National Sports and Cultural Center, 123
Natural Park of the Our Valley, 37
Natural Park of the Upper Sûre, 22, 37, *37*
natural resources map, *69*
Nazis, *47*
Nenghis Hiel cave, 24
New Wine Festival, 105
New Year's holiday, 107, 127
North Atlantic Treaty Organization (NATO), 50
Nospelt, 106
Notre Dame Cathedral, *13*, 60, 96, *98*, 99
Nut Market, 105

O

Octave devotional, 100
Oesling region. *See* Ardennes region.
Old Fish Market, 60
Old Luxembourg City, *116*
old-growth forests, 30–31
"Ons Héemécht" (Michel Lentz), 112
Oude Biezen Castle, *10*
Our River, 18, 25, 34
Ozaukee County Pioneer Village, 83

P

Parc Merveilleux, 124
Parc Naturel de la Haute-Sûre, 37, *37*
Parliament, 55, *55*, 56, 57, 87
passenger trains, 72–73, *73*
Patton, George, 49
Pei, I. M., 109–110, *109*
people
    education, 9–10, *9*, 48, 86, 88, 114–115
    emigration, 81–82, *82*, 83
    ethnic diversity of, 77
    housing, 118–119, *119*
    immigrants, 14, 79–81, 82, 85
    languages, 9–10, 40, 84–87, *84*, 87–89
    literacy rate, 114
    names, 14
population, 78, 81, 82
Pétange, 46, 78, 79
Pétrusse River, 61
Pétrusse Valley, 29, 61
pheasants, 34, *34*
Place d'Armes, *46*, 60, *78*
Place Guillaume, 122
Place Guillaume II, 60
plant life
    broom flowers, 31, *31*
    conifers, 30
    deciduous trees, 30

flowers, 30
    Grünwald forest, 31
    old-growth forests, 30–31
    trees, 30–31, *30*
    wildflowers, 31
poinsettias, 106, *107*
polecats, 33–34
Pont Grand-Duchesse Charlotte
    (bridge), 61
population density map, *79*
prime ministers, 56–57, *57*
Protestants, 92

Q

Quereinhaus, 119

R

Radio Luxembourg, 74
Radio Télévision Luxembourg (RTL)
    Group, 74–75, *74*
Radwanderwege bike paths, 121
rail lines, 72–73
Räuberhöle cave, 24
regional government, 59
religion
    abbeys, 22, 95
    archbishops, 95
    Benedictine abbey, 22
    Calvinists, 92
    Church of Saint Laurent, 23
    constitution and, 91
    convents, 95
    Greek Orthodox Church, 92–93
    holidays, 93–94
    Judaism, 93
    Lutherans, 92
    monasteries, 95
    Muslims, 92, *92*
    orders, 95–96

Roman Catholic Church, 13, 40,
   91, *91*, 92, *92*, *99*
Russian Orthodox Church, 92–93
Serbian Orthodox Church, 92–93
Springprozession, 100–101, *100*, *101*
Te Deum (mass), 105
Renewig, Guy, 113
roadways, 71
Robert Schuman Center for European
   Studies and Research, 50
Rock of Gibraltar, 43
Rodange, Michel, 112
Roman Catholic Church, 13, 40,
   91, 92
Roman Empire, 10, 39–40, 87
Route du Vin, 23
Russian Orthodox Church, 92–93

S

Saint Donatus, Iowa, 83, *83*
Saint John's Church, 99
Saint Laurent church, 97
Saint Martin of Dudelange church, 98
Saint Maurice abbey, 97
Saint Nicholas Day, 126
Saint Stephen's Day, 94
Saint Vitus's dance, 101
Schoenfels castle, 45
Schueberfouer festival, 43, 61, 105
Schuman Plan, 50
Schuman, Robert, 50, *50*, 133
Septfontaine's castle, 45
Serbian Orthodox Church, 92–93
Shadow of the Vampire (film), 113, *113*
Shrove Monday, 93
Shrove Tuesday, 93
Siegfried, count of Ardennes, 40–41,
   60, 61, 133
Sigismund (emperor), 43

Société Européenne des Satellites
   (SES) Global, 75, *75*
sports, 120–123, *120*
Springprozession, 100–101, *100*, *101*
Stations of the Cross, 93
steel industry, 14, 46, 65–66, *65*
Steichen, Edward, 22, 110, 111,
   111, 133
Stephen (saint), 94, *94*
Sunnen House, 83
Superior Court of Justice, 58
Sûre River, 18, 25, *25*, *28*
Sûre River valley, 24

T

Tageblatt/Zeitung fir Lëtzebuerg
   newspaper, 75
Te Deum (Mass), 105
topographical map, *18*
Tour de France, 121
tourism, 19, 22
towns. *See also* cities; villages.
   Clervaux, 22
   Diekirch, 23, 39, 97
   Durbuy, *26*
   Echternach, 23, *23*, 100, *103*, 108
   Vianden, 22, *22*, 98, 105
   Wiltz, 23, 30, 108
transportation, 71–73, *71*, *72*, *73*
Treaty on European Union, 51
trees, 30–31, *30*
Treveri tribe, 39
Troisvierges, 98
Tudor accumulator, 67
Tudor, Henry, 67

U

Union of European Football
   Associations (UEFA), 120

United Nations (UN), 50
University Center, 115
University of Luxembourg, *115*

V

Valley of the Seven Castles, 45
Veidt (fiddling thief), 101
Vianden, 22, *22*, 98, 105
Vianden castle, 19, *22*
villages. *See also* cities; towns.
   Esch-sur-Sûre, 22, 23, *29*, 37
   Hamm, 49
   Nospelt, 106
   Troisvierges, 98
vineyards, 21, 27, *27*, 69, *69*

W

watersports, 121
waterways, 24–26
weights and measures, 65
Wenceslas II (emperor), 43
Whit Sunday, 94, 100
Whit Tuesday, 100
White Ernz valley, 24
wild boar, 32, *32*
wildflowers, 31
wildlife. *See* animal life; plant life;
   insect life.
William I, king of the Netherlands, 44
Willibrord (saint), 23, 96, *96*, 100,
   101, 133
Wiltz, 23, 30, 108
Wine Trail, 23
winemaking, 11, 21, 23, 69, 105
World War I, 47, 111
World War II, 23, 41, 47–48, 48–49,
   48, 85
Wormeldange, 105

Meet the Author

Ann Heinrichs fell in love with faraway places while reading Doctor Doolittle books as a child. Now she is trying to cover as much of the earth as possible. She has traveled through most of the United States and much of Europe, as well as the Middle East, East Asia, and Africa.

Ann grew up roaming the woods of Arkansas. Now she lives in Chicago. She is the author of more than one hundred books for children and young adults on American, European, Asian, and African history and culture. Several of her books have won national and state awards.

Ann says, "To me, writing nonfiction is a bigger challenge than writing fiction. With nonfiction, you can't just dream something up—everything has to be true. Finding out facts is harder than making things up, but to me it's more rewarding. When I uncover the facts, they always turn out to be more spectacular than fiction could ever be. And I'm always on the lookout for what kids in another country are up to, so I can report back to kids here."

Ann has also written numerous newspaper, magazine, and encyclopedia articles. As an advertising copywriter, she has covered everything from plumbing hardware to Oriental rugs. She holds bachelor's and master's degrees in piano performance. More recently, her performing arts are t'ai chi empty-hand and sword forms. She is an award-winning martial artist and participates in regional and national tournaments.

Photo Credits